FRETBOARD ROADMAPS SLIDE GUITAR

THE ESSENTIAL PATTERNS THAT ALL THE PROS KNOW AND USE

CONTENTS

THE RECORDING AND PRACTICE TRACKS

All the licks, riffs and tunes in this book are played on the accompanying audio. There are also five Practice Tracks on the recording. Each track illustrates a specific soloing style, such as "first position slide licks in open G tuning," or "slide in standard tuning in the key of E." They are mixed so that the lead guitar is on one side of your stereo and the backup band is on the other, so you can tune out the lead guitar and practice playing solos with the backup band.

RECORDING CREDITS
Guitar and Vocals—Fred Sokolow
Sound Engineer and Other Instruments—Dennis O'Hanlon
Recorded at O'Hanlon Recording and Music Services

NOTE: This book is a slide guitarist's extension of Fred Sokolow's ***Fretboard Roadmaps*** (Hal Leonard Corporation, HL00696514), which includes even more music theory for guitarists, along with musical examples, solos and licks. We recommend you use ***Fretboard Roadmaps*** as a reference, along with this book.

To access audio visit:
www.halleonard.com/mylibrary

5677-1667-3890-7758

ISBN 978-0-634-00138-3

7777 W. BLUEMOUND RD. P.O. BOX 13819 MILWAUKEE, WI 53213

Visit Hal Leonard Online at
www.halleonard.com

INTRODUCTION

Accomplished slide guitarists can play solos and play backup in any key—all over the fretboard. They know many different soloing approaches and can play slide in a blues, rock, country or pop song. They can play in several open tunings or in standard tuning.

There are moveable patterns on the guitar fretboard that make it easy to do these things. The pros are aware of these "fretboard roadmaps," even if they don't read music. If you want to play electric or acoustic slide with other people, this is essential guitar knowledge.

You need the fretboard roadmaps if...

- All your slide soloing sounds the same and you want variety in your playing.
- Some keys are harder to play in than others.
- You can't automatically play any slide lick you can think or hum.
- You know a lot of slide guitar "bits and pieces," but you don't have a system that ties it all together.

Read on, and many mysteries will be explained. If you're serious about playing slide guitar, the pages that follow can shed light and save you a great deal of time.

Good luck,

Fred Sokolow

PRELIMINARIES

USING A SLIDE

Fret the strings *lightly* with the slide to get a clean sound. Pressing hard produces buzzes and fret noise. Hold the slide straight up and down, parallel to the fretwires, and fret the strings *right over the fretwires,* not between them. Otherwise, your notes will be flat.

MUTING

Some players mute unwanted strings with the fingertips of their picking hand. To eliminate fret noises, others mute the strings behind the slide with one or two fretting fingers.

SEVERAL WAYS TO SLIDE

Besides sliding up to a note, you can slide down from a note, or back and forth between notes. You can also play a series of notes with no sliding, even though you fret them with the slide. All these techniques are illustrated in the following exercise, which is played in standard tuning: 1

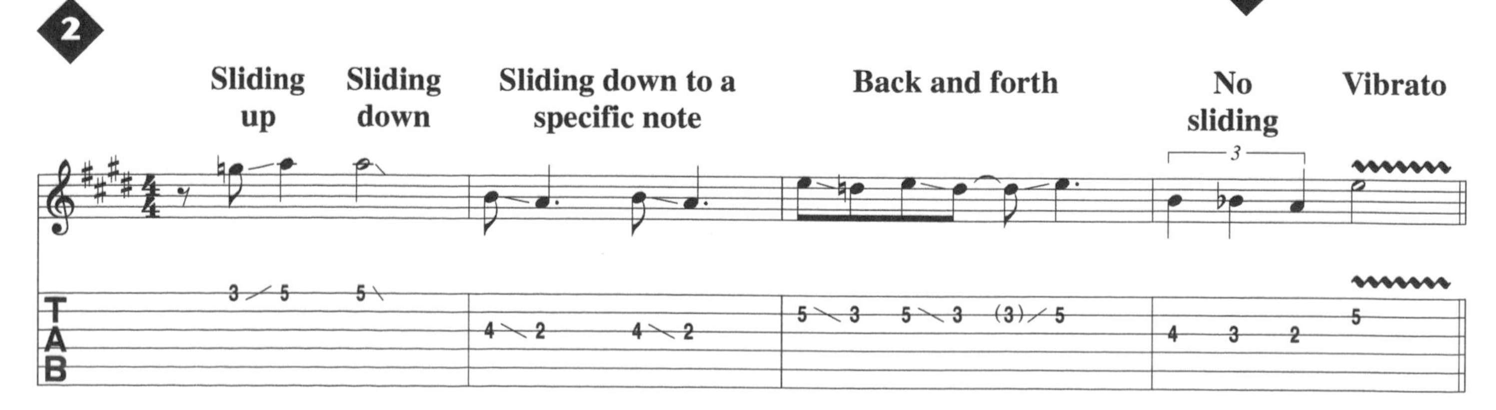

Blues Scale

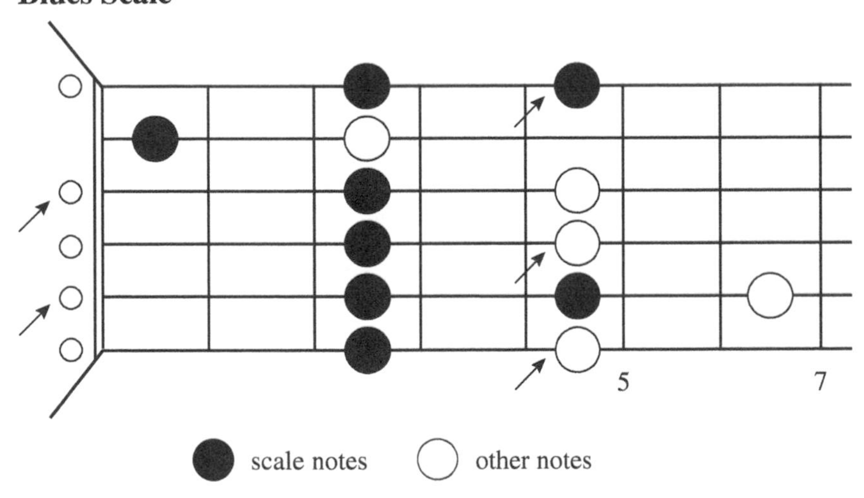

Major Scale

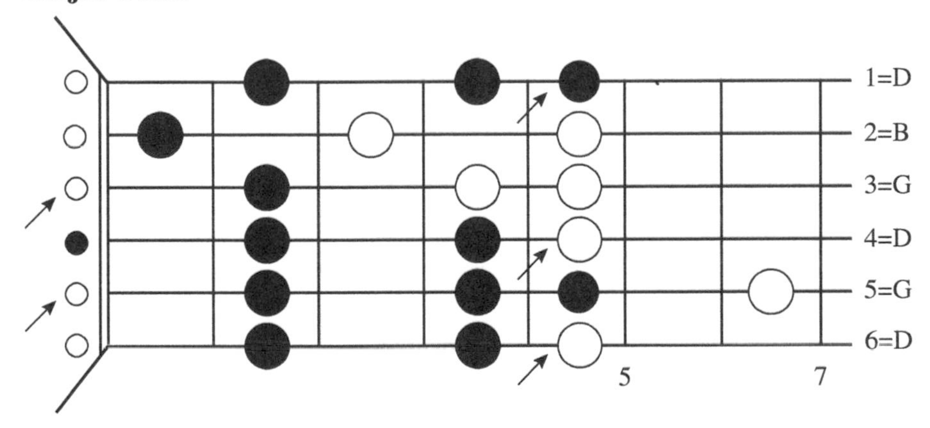

WHY?

- Popularized by Mississippi Delta blues players, G tuning is used by slidesters in rock, blues, R&B, country, folk and gospel music. Once you're familiar with the above scales, you can play countless melodies and licks in first position, in the "open G" tuning.

WHAT?

- ***Both of the above diagrams are for G tuning***. When you strum the open (unfretted) strings in this tuning, you play a G major chord. That's why it's called "open G tuning."
- ***The scales are guidelines.*** Sometimes other notes (between the notes indicated above) work.
- ***The arrows point out the tonic (G) notes***, also called "root" notes. Notice the high tonic note at the 5th fret. A lot of licks will resolve on this note, or on other G notes.
- ***The white dots are "alternates."*** They are duplicated by open strings. For example, the 6th string/5th fret and the open 5th string are both G.

HOW?

- ***To get to G tuning from standard tuning:***
  The 4th (D), 3rd (G) and 2nd (B) strings stay as they are in standard tuning.
  Tune the 6th/E string down two frets, to D. Match it to the open 4th string.
  Tune the 5th/A string down two frets, to G. Match it to the 6th string/5th fret.
  Tune the 1st/E string down two frets, to D. Match it to the 2nd string/3rd fret.

- ***Play the scales ascending and descending, starting from a G note.*** Use your finger, instead of the slide, to fret the strings:

G Tuning
Blues Scale

Major Scale

- ***Play the same scales using the "alternate notes":***

Blues Scale G Tuning

Major Scale

- ***Use the "alternate notes" for sliding or vibrato.*** You can't slide to an open 3rd string/G note, but you can slide up to the same G note at the 4th string/5th fret. You can't play vibrato at the open 1st string/D, but you can play vibrato on the same D note at the 2nd string/3rd fret.

DO IT!

- ***Use the blues scale to ad-lib solos throughout a bluesy tune.*** In spite of the chord changes in "Sliding Rocks," all the soloing is based on the G blues scale.

- ***Vibrato is the wobbling sound that makes the guitar imitate the singing voice.*** To produce an even vibrato, lightly anchor the thumb of your fretting hand against the back of the guitar neck, and wobble the slide back and forth, slightly, from just *behind* the actual note (by a fraction of a fret) to just *in front* of it. This makes the note sing and sustain. The wobble should come from your wrist, not from your arm. In music and tablature, vibrato is indicated by a wiggly line, as in the first bar of "Sliding Rocks."

Sliding Rocks

G Tuning

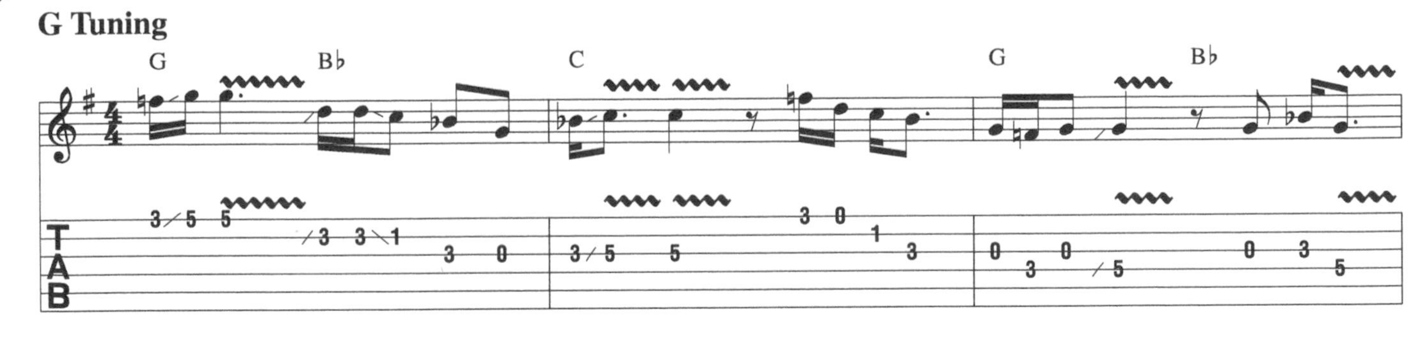

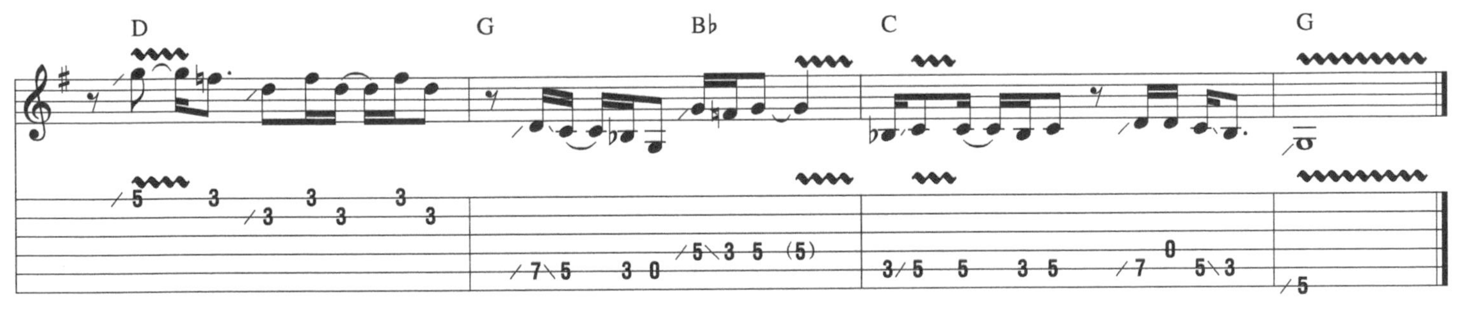

▶ ***Use the blues scale to play melody and blues licks.*** In the following solo, the guitar plays the melody to the old blues, "See, See Rider," including ad-lib blues licks that fill the pauses between melodic phrases.

See, See Rider

Melody

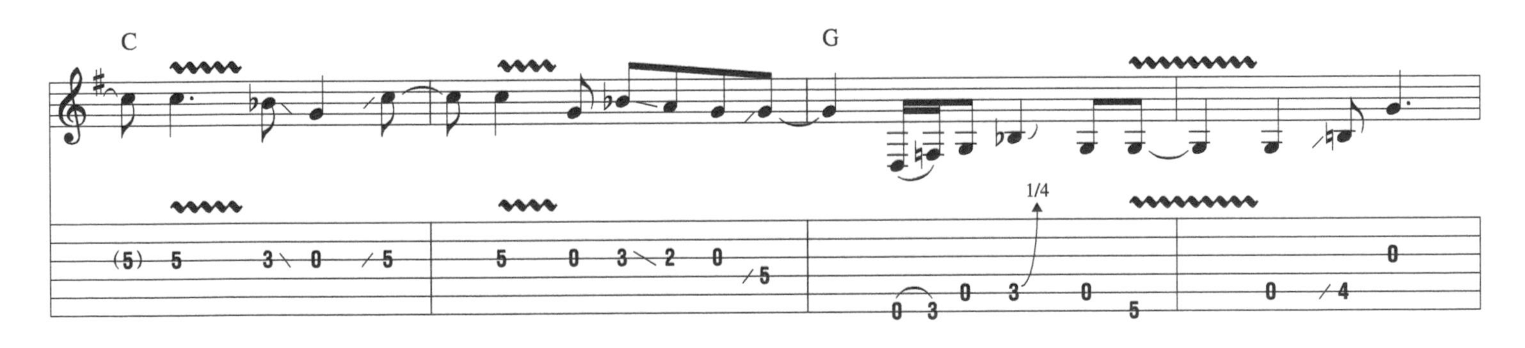

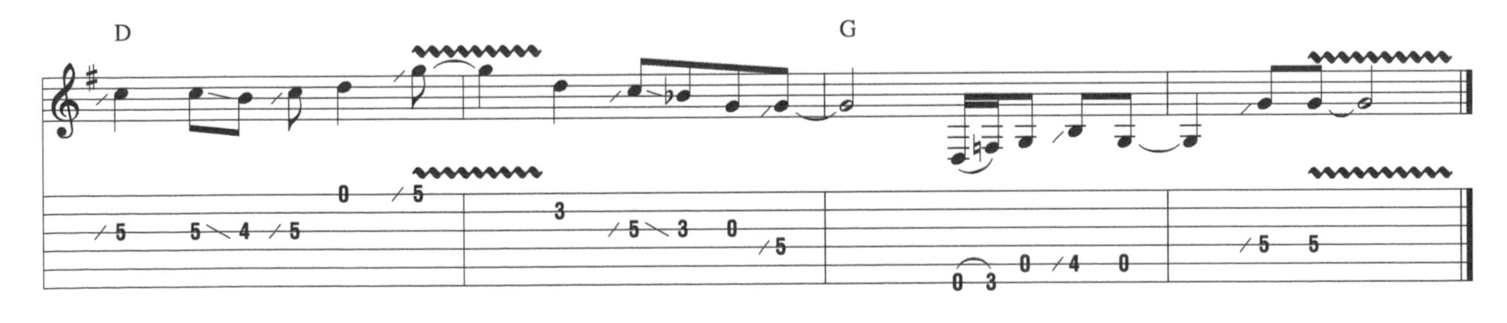

▶ ***Use the major scale to play melodies and ad lib solos.*** In "Chilly Winds," below, the melody and fills that follow are based on the major scale.

Chilly Winds

Melody

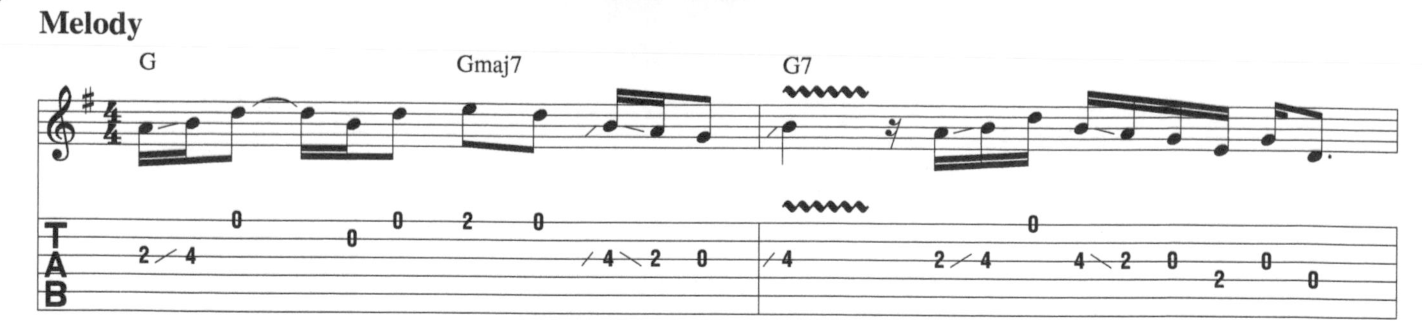

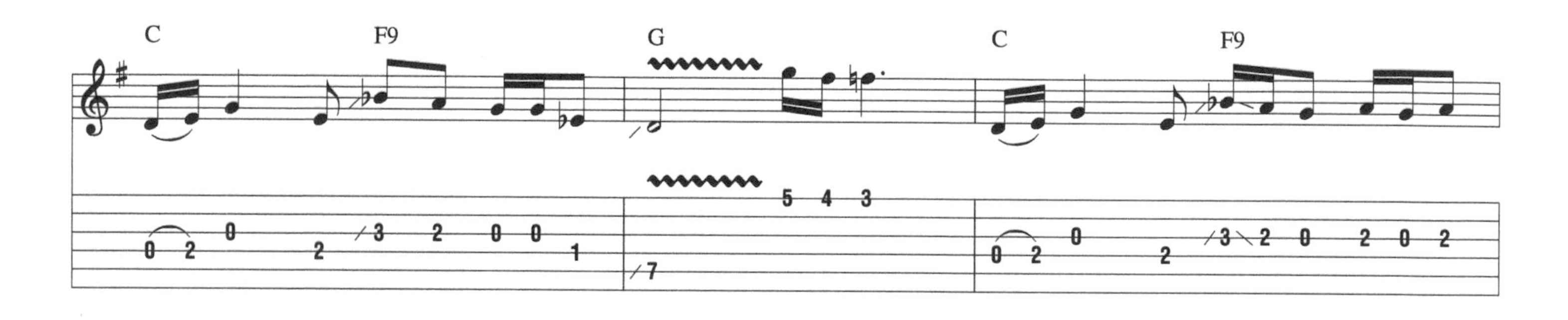

SUMMING UP—NOW YOU KNOW…

▶ ***How to play a first-position G blues scale.***

▶ ***How to play a first-position G major scale.***

▶ ***How to use both scales to play melodies, ad lib solos and licks.***

G TUNING: 12TH FRET SOLOING

Blues Scale

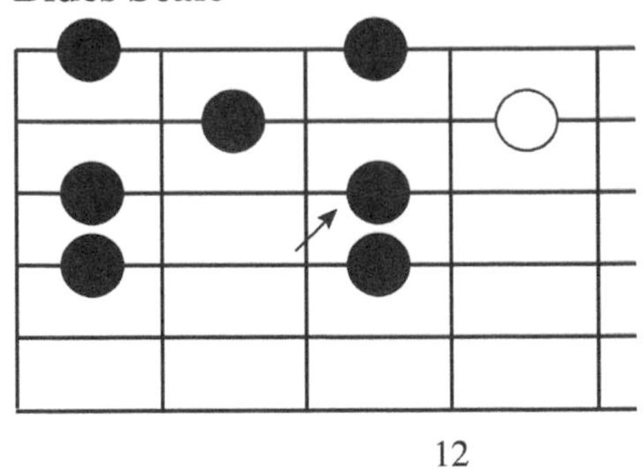

Major Scale

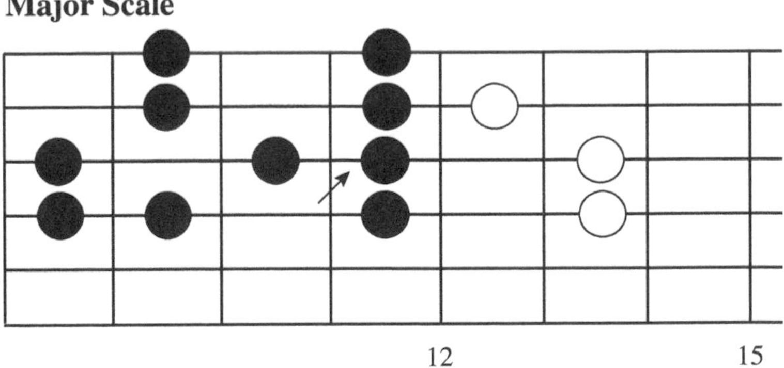

WHY?

- The scales in **ROADMAP #2** make it possible to play tunes in higher registers in the key of G.

WHAT?

- ***As in* ROADMAP #1*, both of the above diagrams are for G tuning.*** The arrows point out the tonic (G) notes.
- ***Only the top four strings are used;*** for lower notes, most players go to first position (as in **ROADMAP #1**).
- ***The white dots are "alternates."*** They are duplicated by lower notes. For example, the 4th string/14th fret and the 3rd string/9th fret are both E.

HOW?

- ***Play the scales ascending and descending, starting from a G note.*** Use your finger, instead of the slide, to fret the strings:

Blues Scale

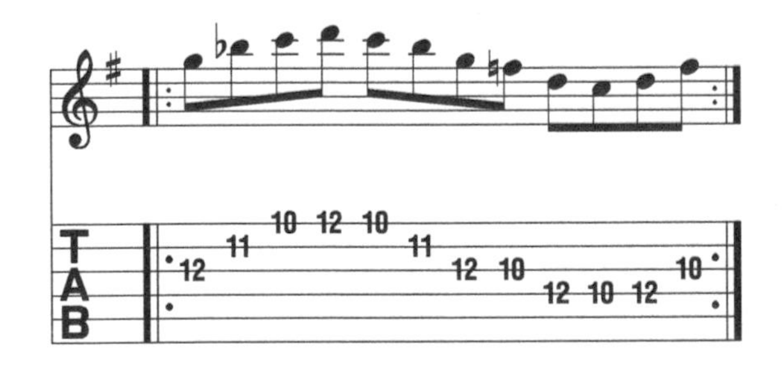

Major Scale

You can also use the "alternate notes":

Blues Scale

Major Scale

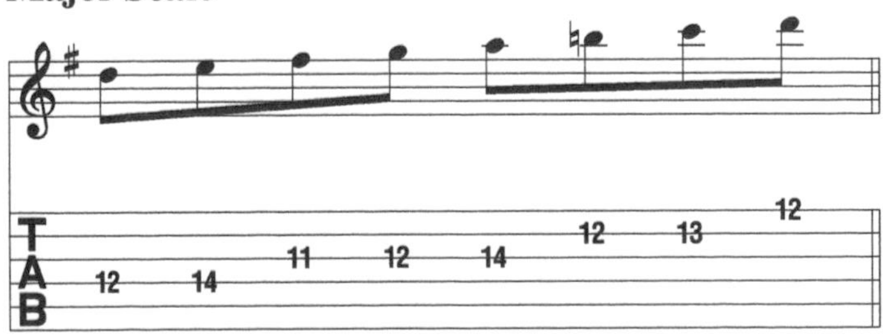

DO IT!

► ***Use the 12th fret blues scale to ad lib solos to bluesy tunes*** like "Sliding Rocks," from **ROADMAP #1**.

7 Sliding Rocks II (at 12th Fret)

G Tuning

► ***Use the 12th fret blues scale to play bluesy melodies*** like "See, See Rider," below:

8 See, See Rider II (at 12th Fret)

G Tuning

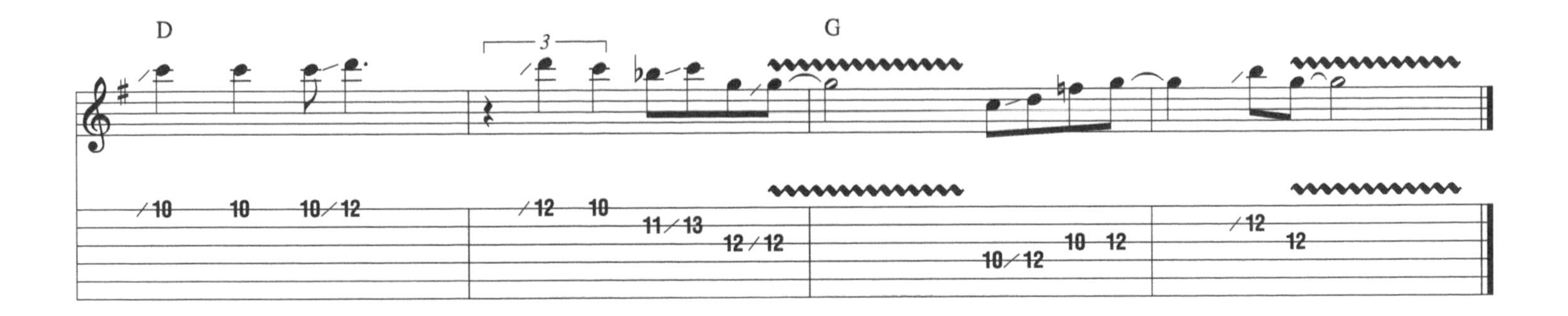

▶ ***Use the 12th fret major scale to play melodies and solos.*** Here's a melodic solo to "Chilly Winds."

Chilly Winds II (at 12th Fret)

G Tuning
Melody

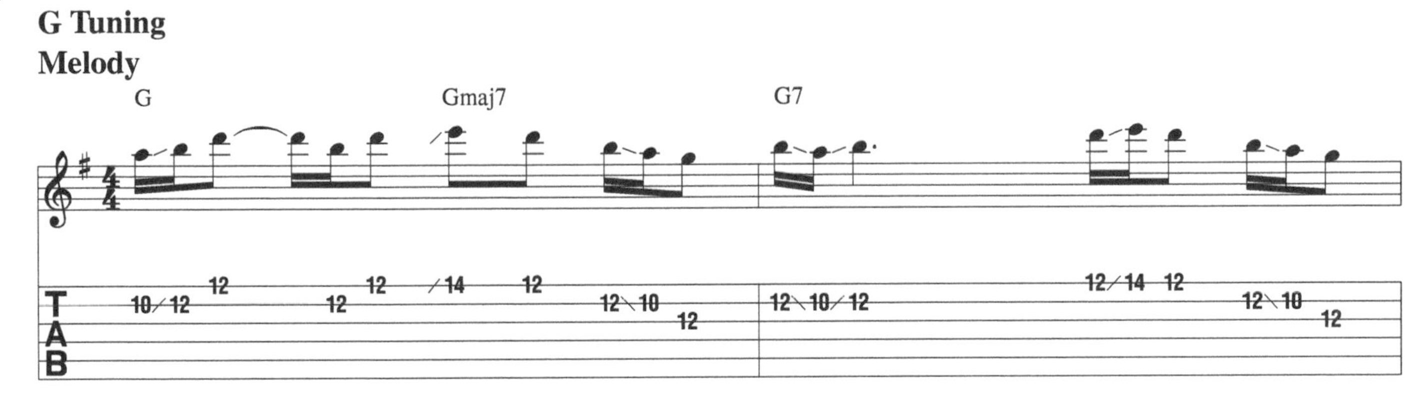

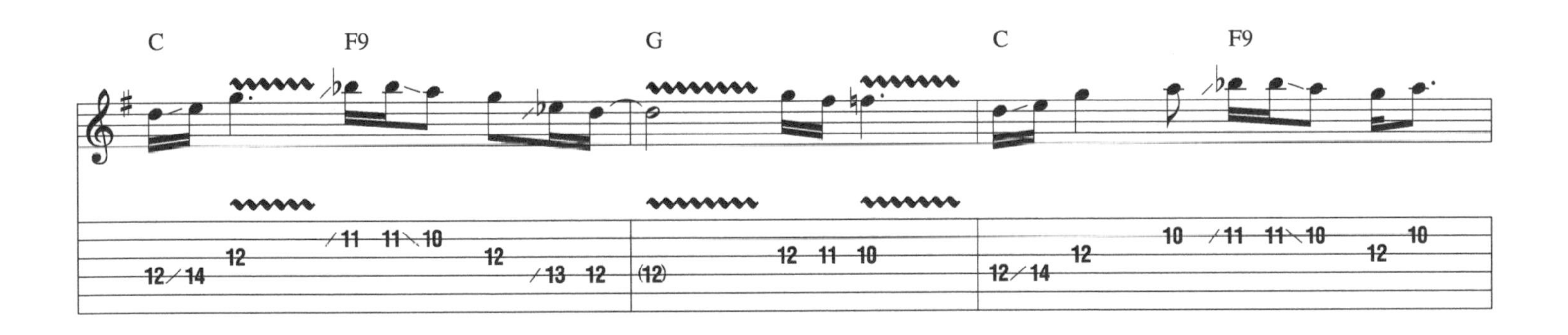

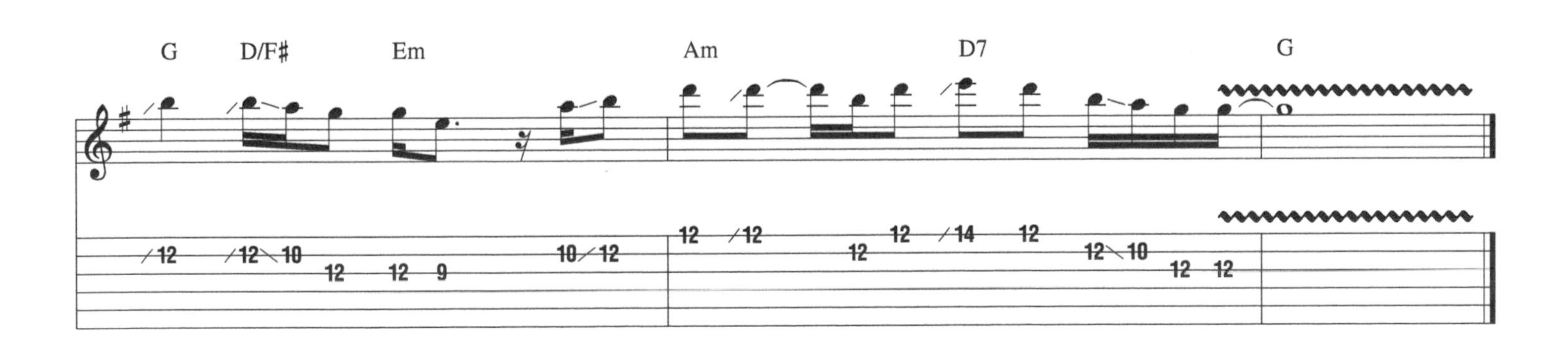

▶ ***Move the 12th fret blues scale to other locations, to play in other keys.*** You can ad lib solos in C, using the same position at the 5th fret, as in the key-of-C version of "See, See Rider" that follows:

See, See Rider III (Key of C)

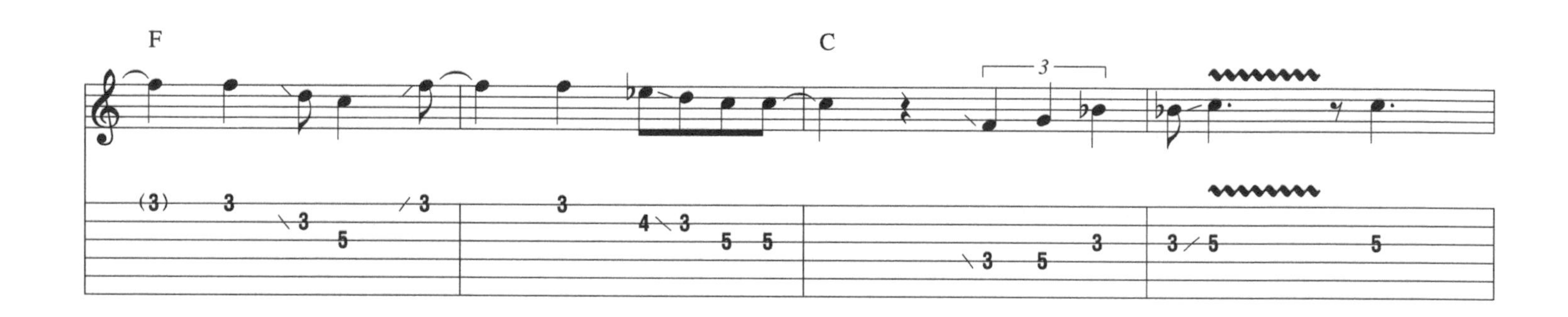

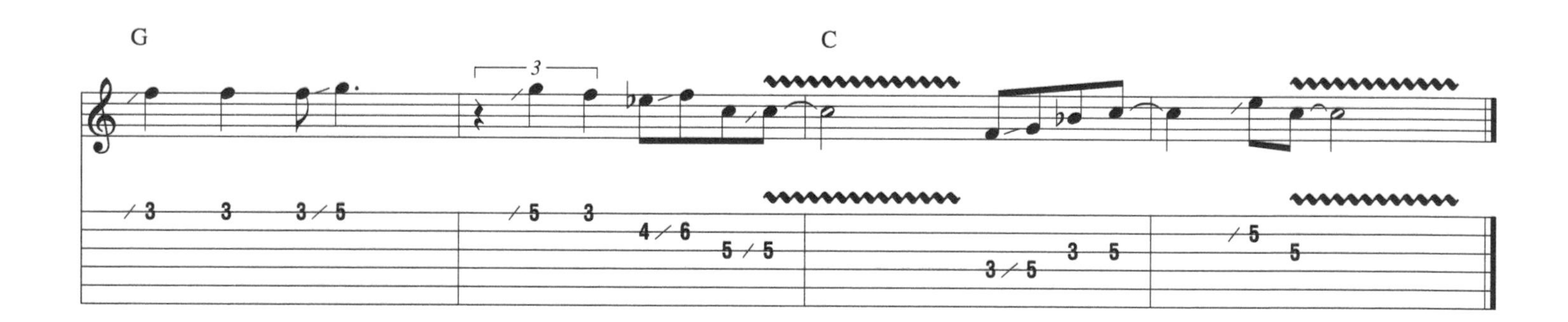

SUMMING UP—NOW YOU KNOW...

▶ ***How to play a G blues scale at the 12th fret.***

▶ ***How to play a G major scale at the 12th fret.***

▶ ***How to use both scales to play melodies, ad lib solos and licks.***

▶ ***How to use the scales to play in keys other than G, while in G tuning.***

#3 G TUNING: BARRED CHORDS

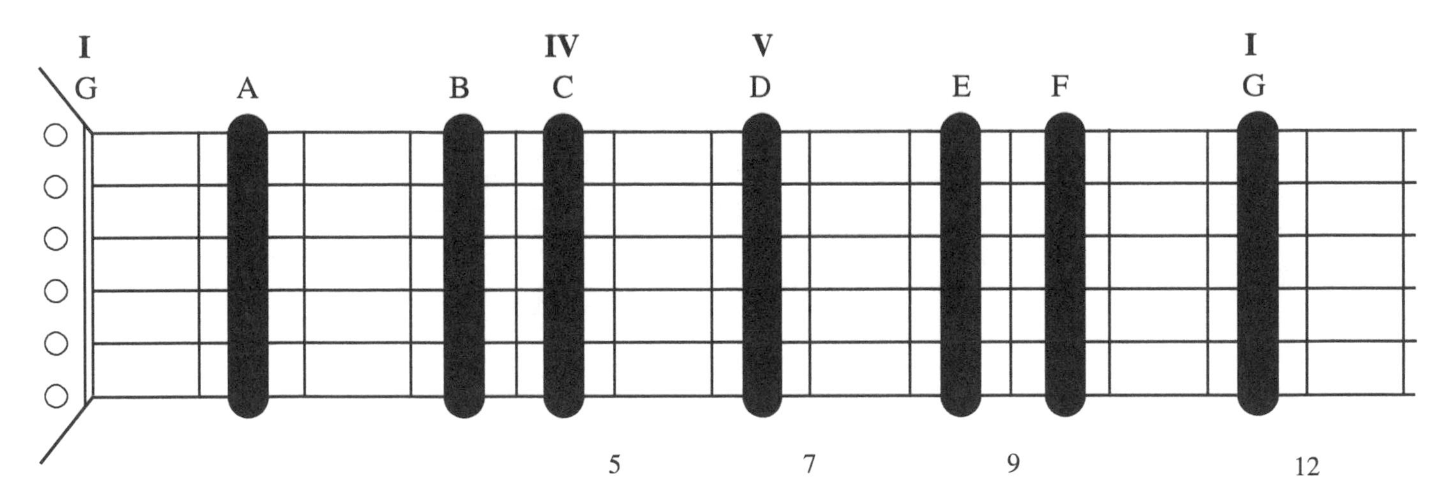

WHY?

- You can base solos and backup on barred chords, which are easy to play with a slide.

WHAT?

- **ROADMAP #3** ***shows the barred chords in G tuning.***
- ***Barre the indicated major chords with a slide or your index finger.*** Barre all six strings or any combination of two, three, four or five strings.
- ***The sharp and flat major chords are between the indicated chords.*** A barre at the 6th fret, one fret above C, is C♯. A barre at the 8th fret, one fret below E, is E♭.
- ***The I (G) IV (C) and V (D) chords are the main three chords in countless songs in the key of G.***
    - The I chord is the tonic (G, in the key of G).
    - The IV chord is so named because its root is the 4th note of the major scale of the given key. (C is the 4th note of the G major scale.) The IV chord is always five frets above the I chord.
    - The V chord is so named because its root is the 5th note of the major scale of the given key. It is always two frets above the IV chord (seven frets above the tonic).
- ***The fretboard "starts over" at the 12th fret.*** The G barre at the 12th fret matches the open string G chord; the 14th fret/A chord matches the 2nd fret/A, and so on.

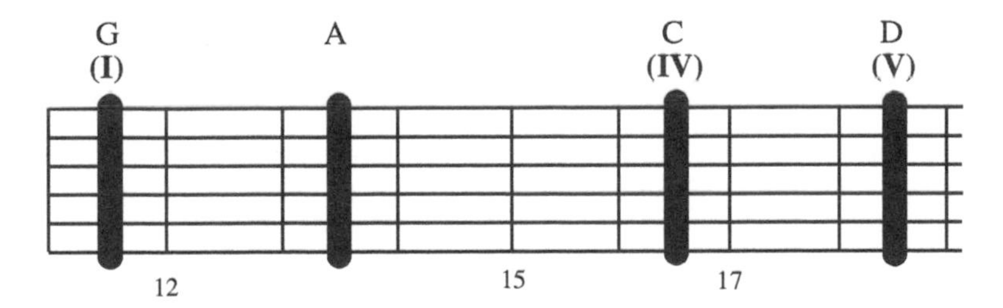

HOW?

- ***You can play chord-based licks and melodies by following a song's chord changes,*** playing the appropriate barred chords.
- ***Besides playing the barred notes, you can play major scale and blues scale notes*** like those described in **ROADMAP #2**:

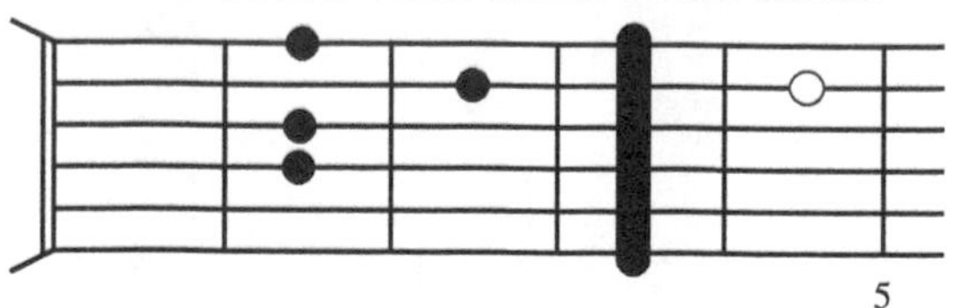

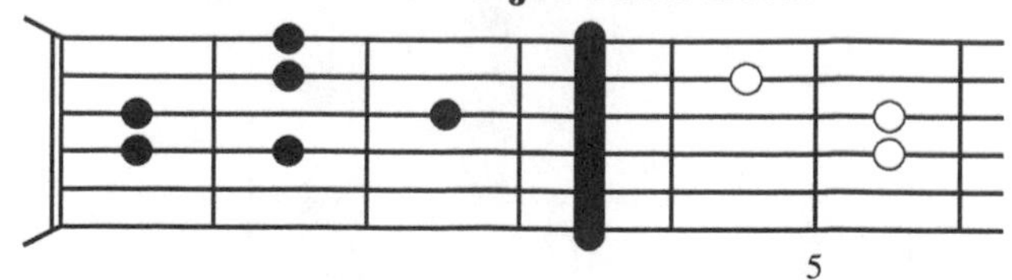

- ***The 1st and 2nd strings, three frets above a barre, make a 7th chord:***

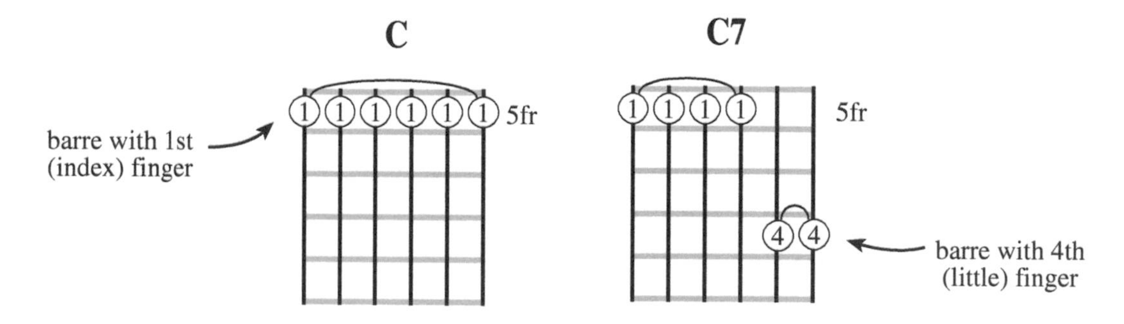

- ***The 1st string, five frets above a barre, is a high tonic note.*** (The 1st string/10th fret, five frets above the C barre, is a high C note.) This "key note" is often useful in solos.

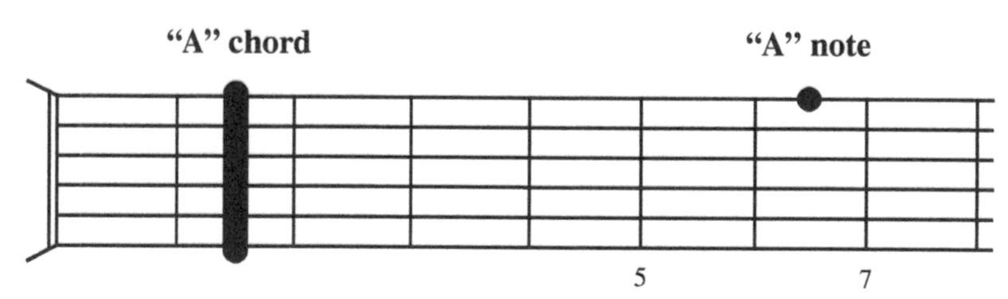

- ***You can locate minor chords by relating them to barre chords, as shown in the chart below, which indicates D minor chords:***

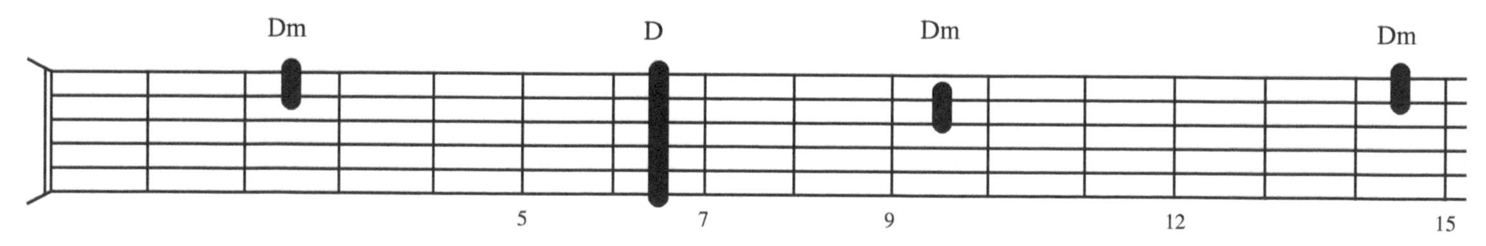

- There's a Dm on the 1st and 2nd strings, four frets below the barre D, or eight frets above the barre.

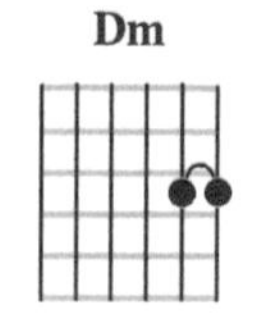

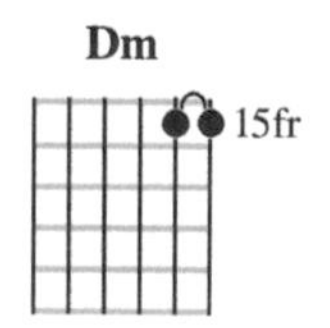

▶ There's a Dm on the 2nd and 3rd strings, three frets above the barre D.

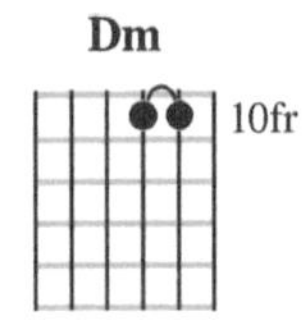

DO IT!

▶ ***Play backup and melody to "Stagolee" by barring the song's chords:***

11

Stagolee

► ***Play chord-based backup to "The Water is Wide,"*** which has many chord changes, major and minor.

The Water Is Wide

12

G Tuning

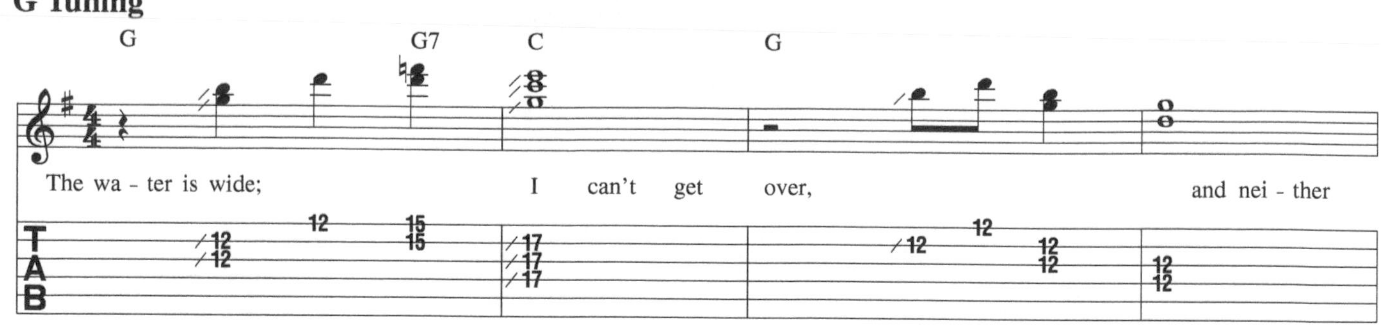

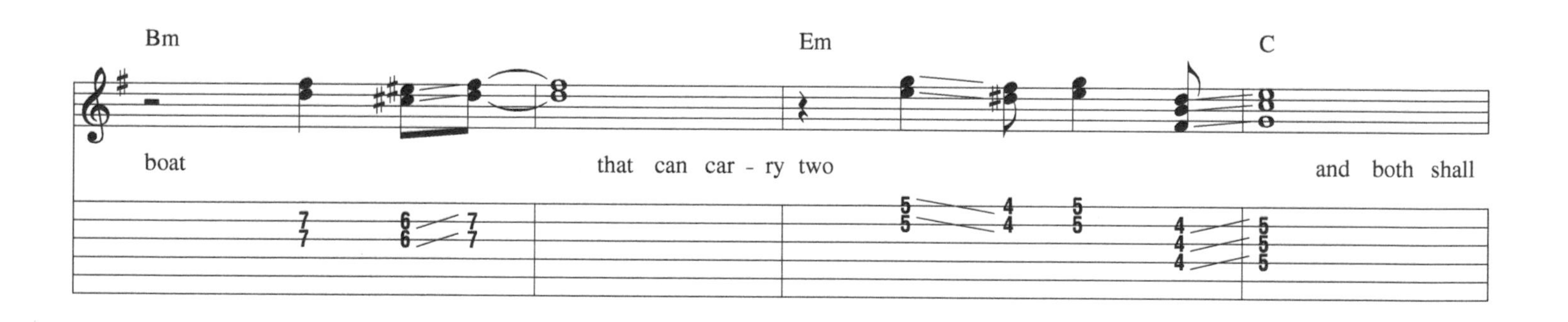

▶ ***You can play chord-based solos in other keys, while tuned to open G,*** by using the licks and ideas in the last several tunes. The solo to the following funk/rock tune in F is a good example:

Funky Riff

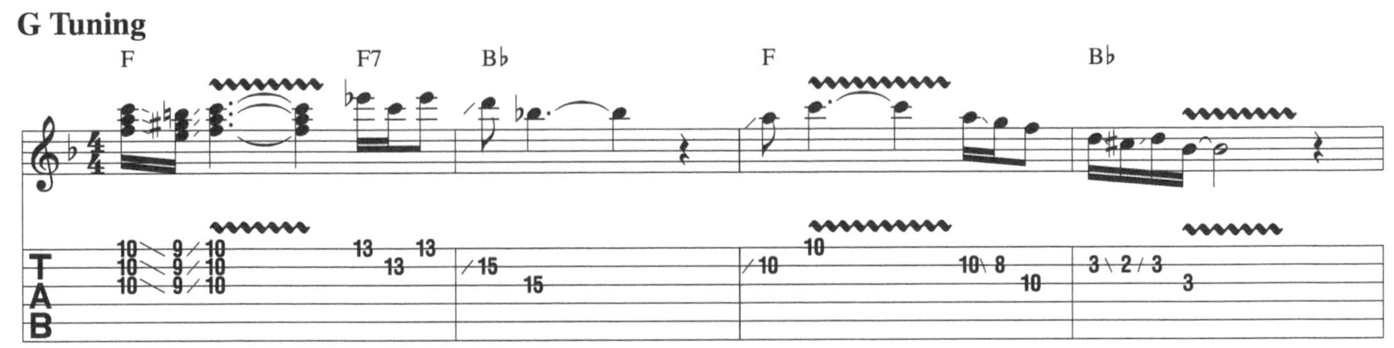

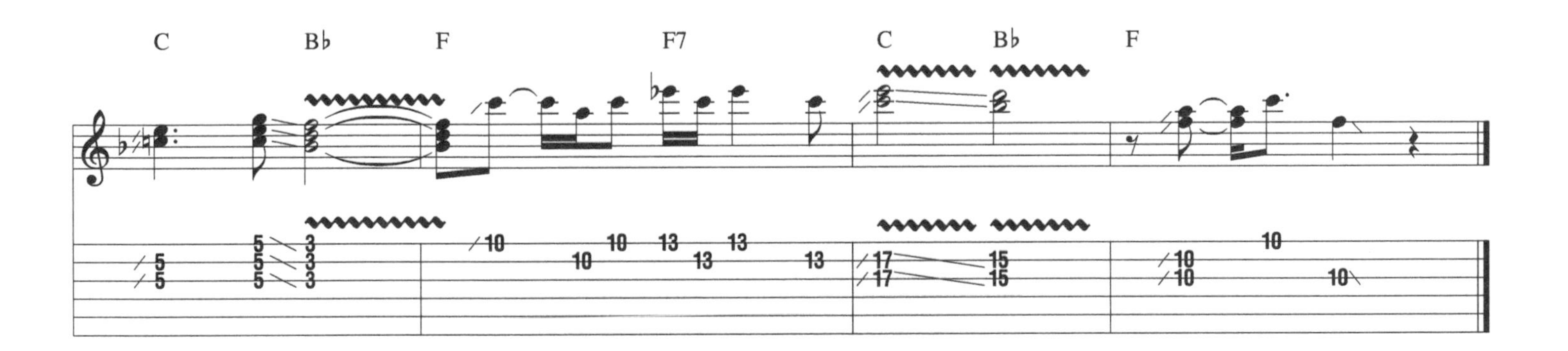

SUMMING UP—NOW YOU KNOW…

▶ ***How to play all the barred major chords in G tuning.***

▶ ***How to make the barred major chords into 7ths.***

▶ ***How to make the barred major chords into minors.***

▶ ***How to play chord-based solos and backup in G tuning.***

▶ ***How to play chord-based solos and backup in keys other than G, in G tuning.***

D TUNING: FIRST POSITION

Blues Scale

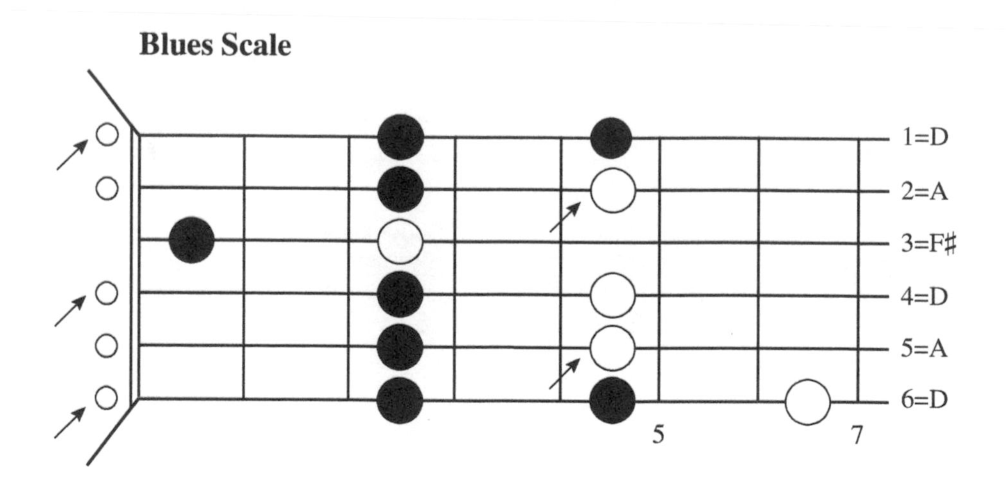

Major Scale

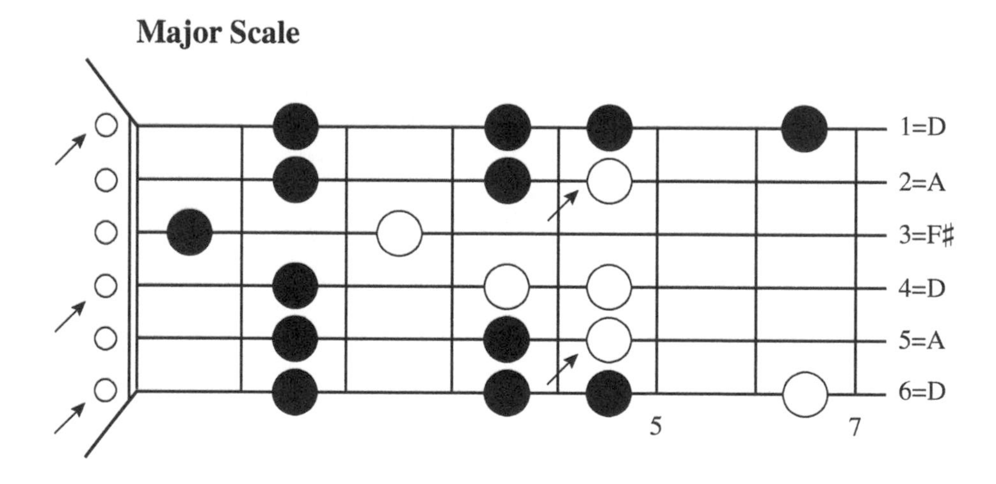

WHY?

- Like G tuning, D tuning is a popular Delta blues tuning that has been co-opted by guitarists of all musical genres. The major and blues scales above help you play tunes in first position/open D.

WHAT?

- ***Both of the above diagrams are for D tuning.*** When you strum the open (unfretted) strings in this tuning, you play a D major chord. The tonic note is on the top (1st string) and bottom (6th string).
- ***The scales are guidelines.*** Sometimes other notes (not indicated above) work.
- ***The arrows point out the root (tonic) notes, which are D notes.***
- ***The dots in white are "alternates."*** They are duplicated by open strings. For example, the 2nd string/5th fret and the open 1st string are both D.

HOW?

- ***To get to D tuning from standard tuning:***

  The 4th (D) and 5th (A) strings stay as they are in standard tuning.
  Tune the 6th/E string down two frets, to D. Match it to the open 4th string.
  Tune the 3rd/G string down one fret, to F#. Match it to the 4th string/4th fret.
  Tune the 2nd/B string down two frets, to A. Match it to the open 5th string.
  Tune the 1st/E string down two frets, to D. Match it to the open 4th string.

- ***Play the scales ascending and descending, starting from a D note.*** Use your finger, instead of the slide, to fret the strings:

Blues Scale
D Tuning

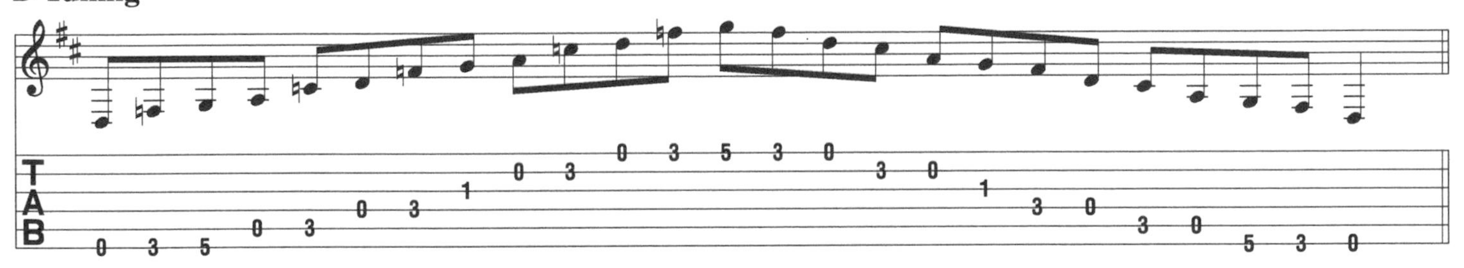

Major Scale
D Tuning

- ***Play the same scales using the "alternate notes":***

Blues Scale
D Tuning

Major Scale
D Tuning

DO IT!

▶ ***Use the D blues scale to ad-lib solos throughout a bluesy tune*** like this rock tune, "Detox":

▶ ***Use the blues scale to play melody and blues licks.*** In "So Long," the guitar plays ad-lib "fills" during the pauses in the vocal line; then it plays a melodic solo.

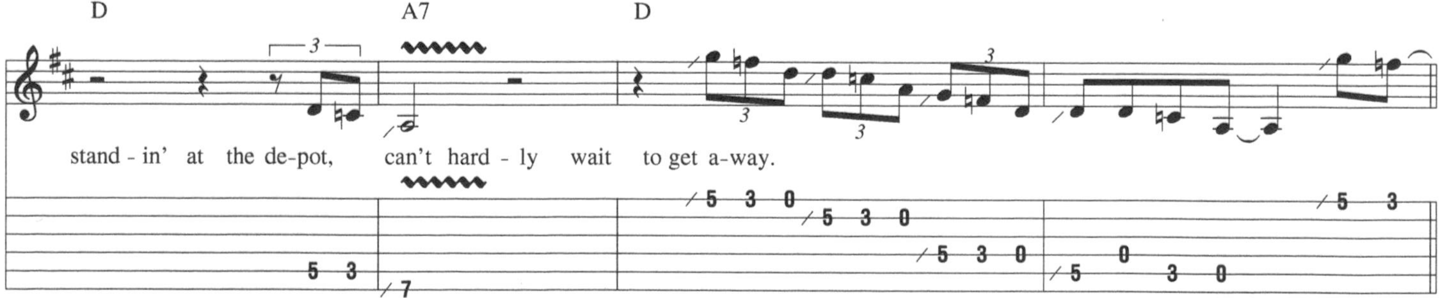

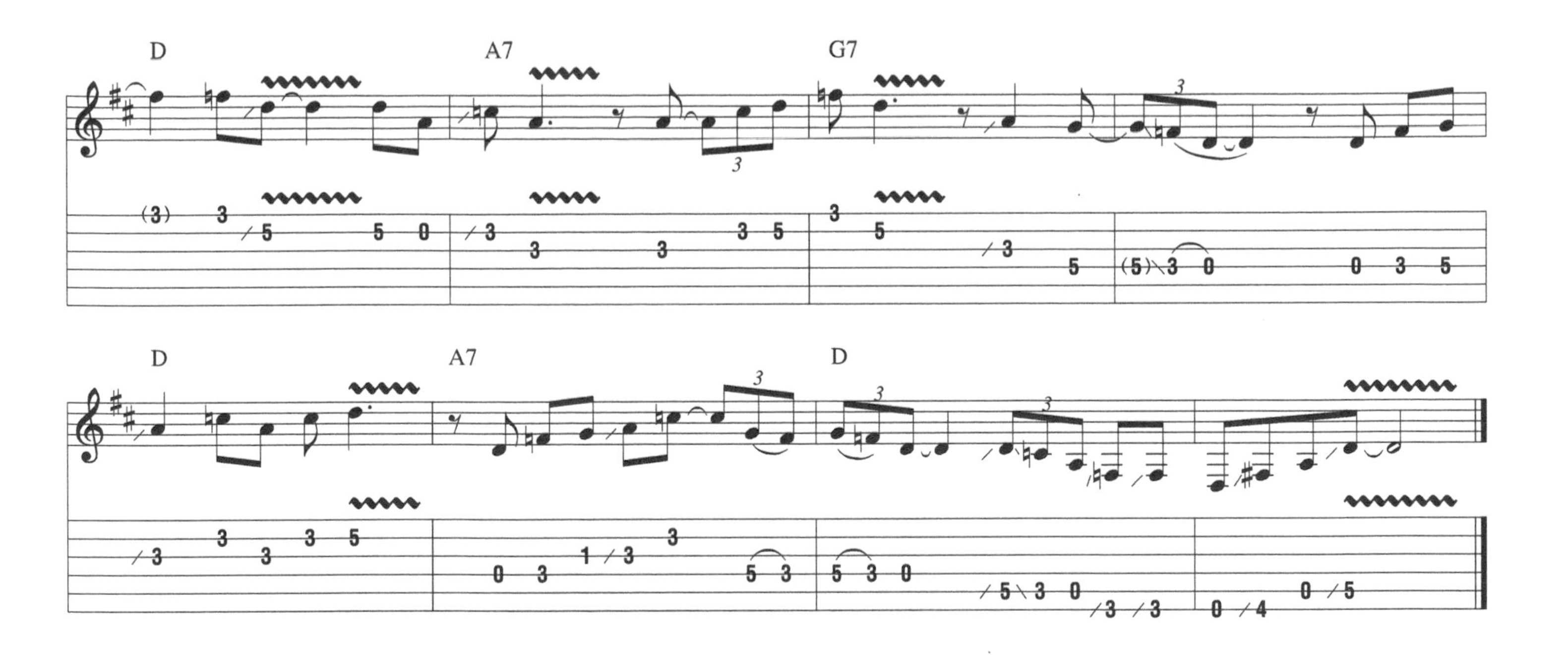

▶ ***Use the D major scale to play melodies and ad lib solos or licks.*** In "Careless Love," below, the guitar plays the melody and a few fills.

17

Careless Love

D Tuning

SUMMING UP—NOW YOU KNOW…

▶ ***How to play a first-position D blues scale.***

▶ ***How to play a first-position D major scale.***

▶ ***How to use both scales to play melodies, and ad lib solos and licks.***

D TUNING: 12TH FRET SOLOING

Blues Scale

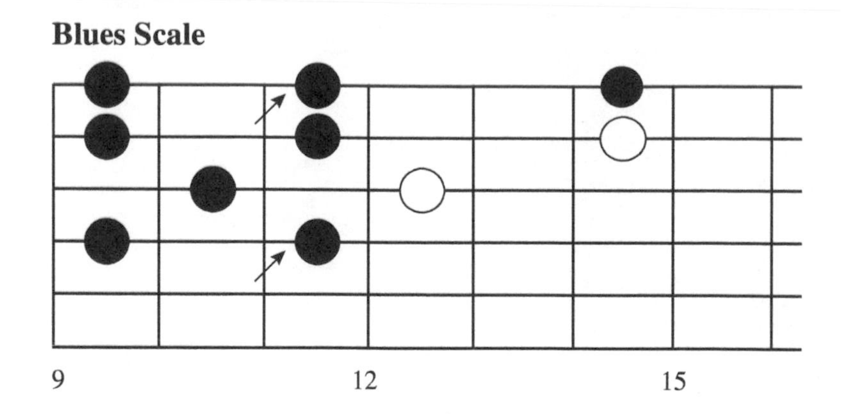

Major Scale

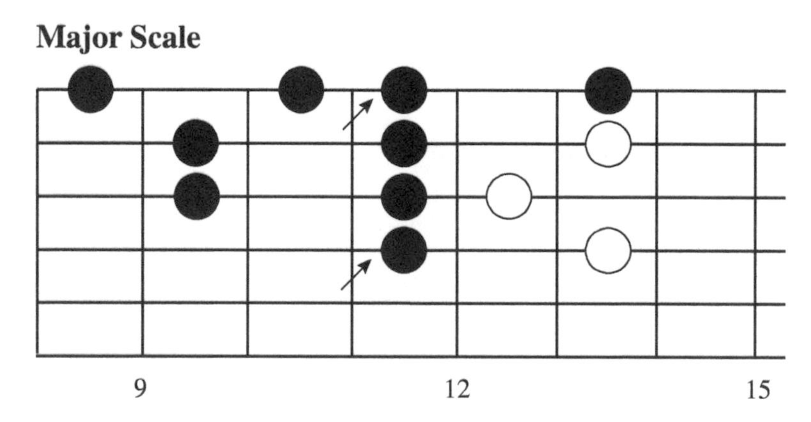

WHY?

- The scales in this roadmap make it possible to play in higher registers in the key of D.

WHAT?

- ***The above blues and major scales are for D tuning.***

HOW?

- ***Play the scales ascending and descending, starting from a 4th string/D note.*** Use the slide to fret the strings:

Blues Scale
D Tuning

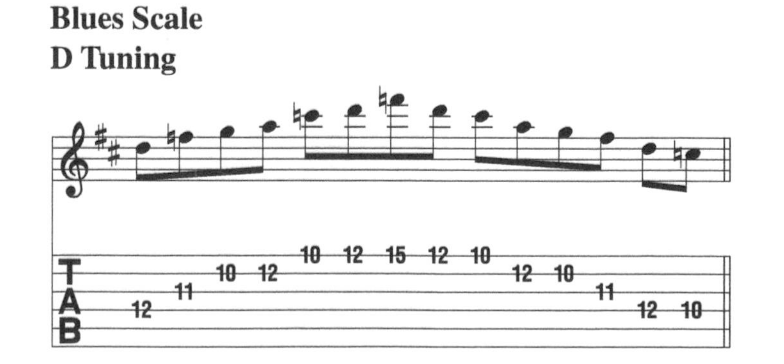

Blues Scale
with Alternate Notes

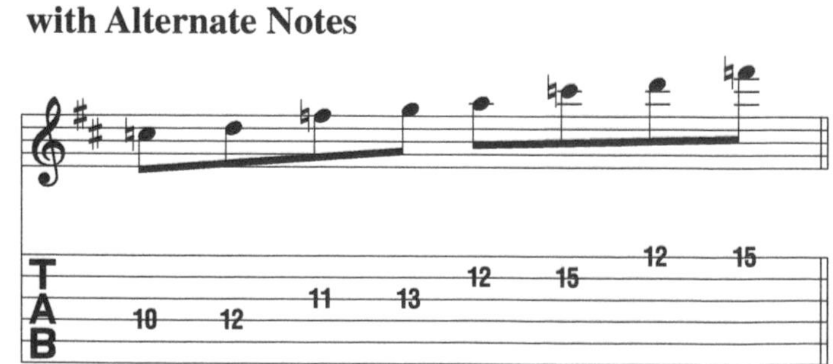

Major Scale
D Tuning

Major Scale
with Alternate Notes

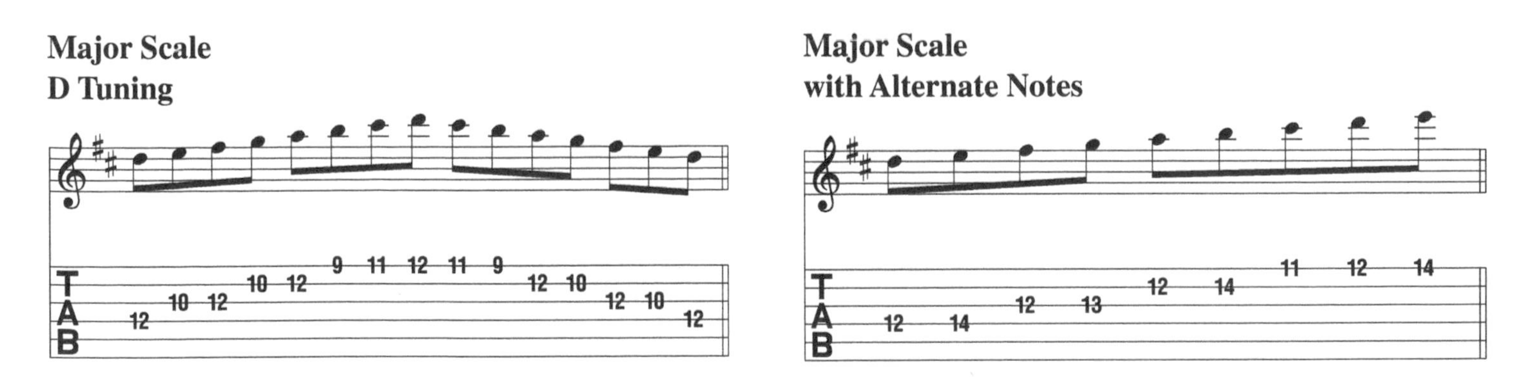

DO IT!

▶ ***Use the D 12th fret blues scale to ad lib solos to bluesy tunes*** like "Twelve O'Clock":

18

Twelve O'Clock

D Tuning

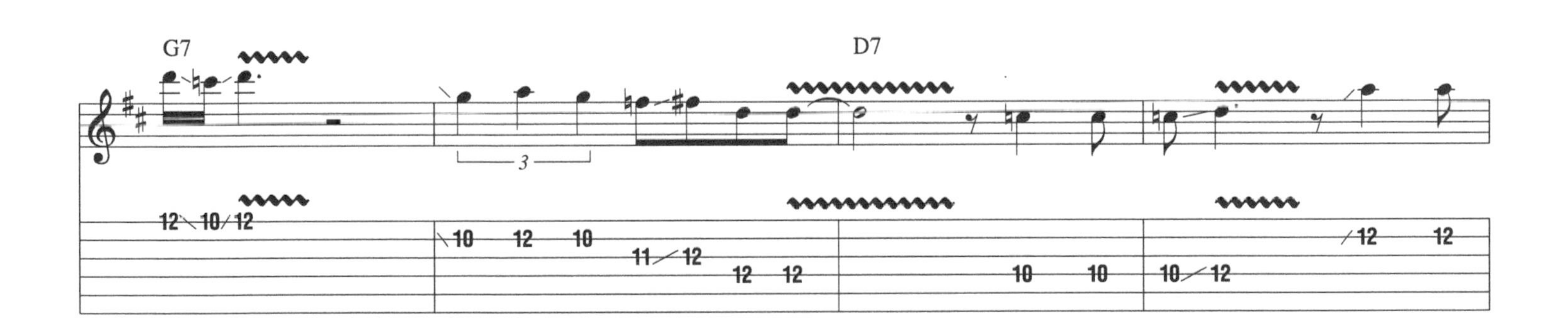

► ***Use the D 12th fret blues scale to play bluesy melodies*** like "See, See Rider":

See, See Rider IV (in D)

D Tuning

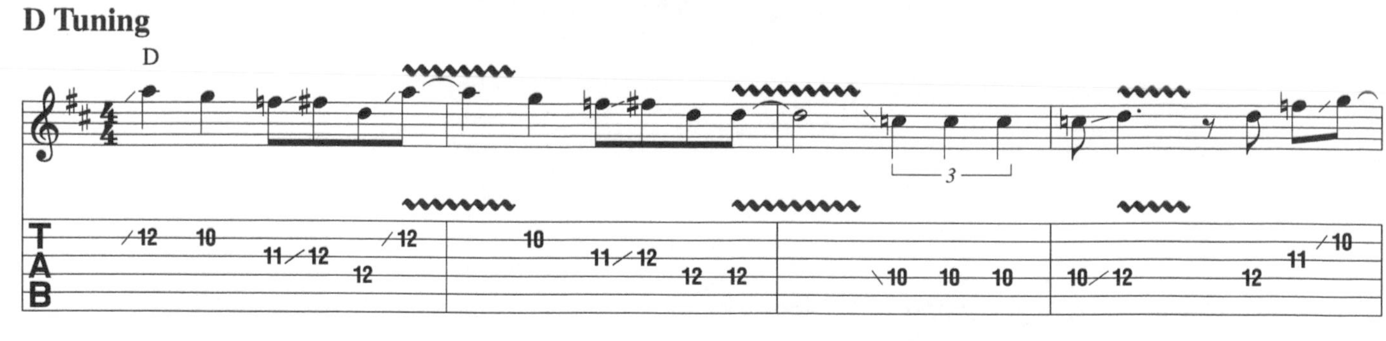

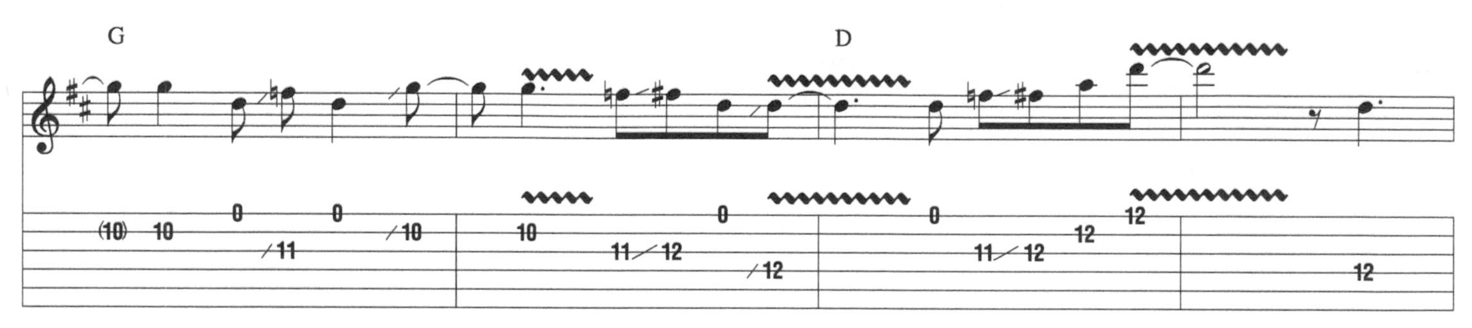

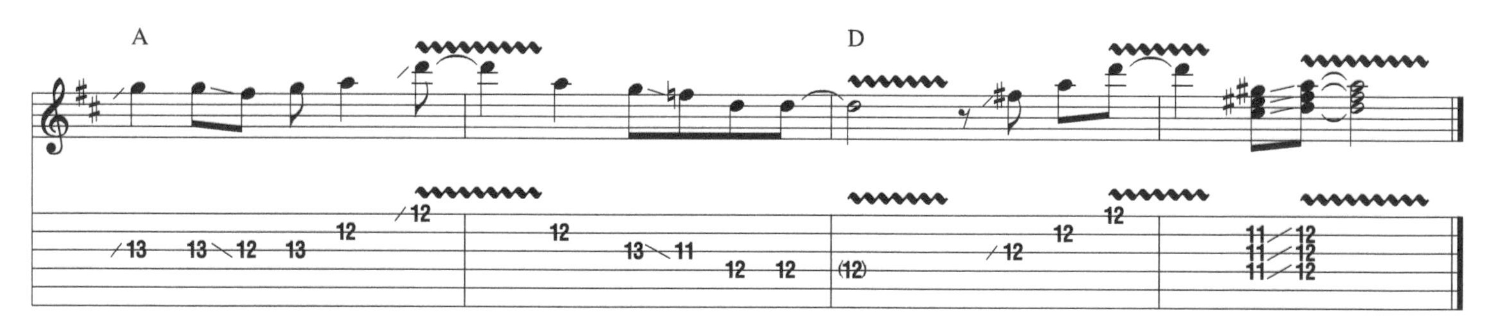

► ***Use the D 12th fret major scale to play melodies and solos.*** Here's a melodic solo to "Frankie and Johnny." Although the old folk tune is a 12-bar blues, its melody is based on the major scale.

20

Frankie and Johnny

D Tuning

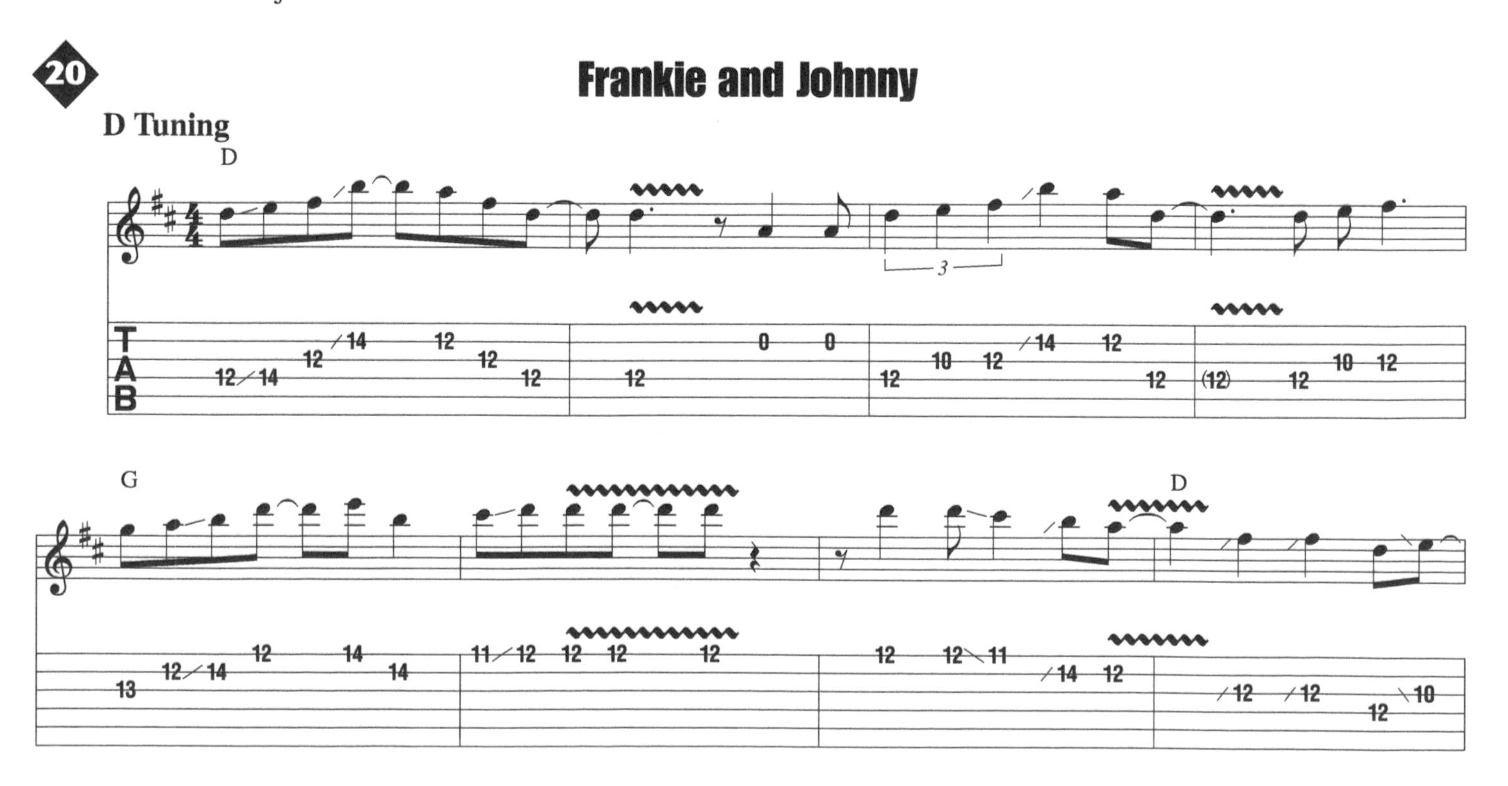

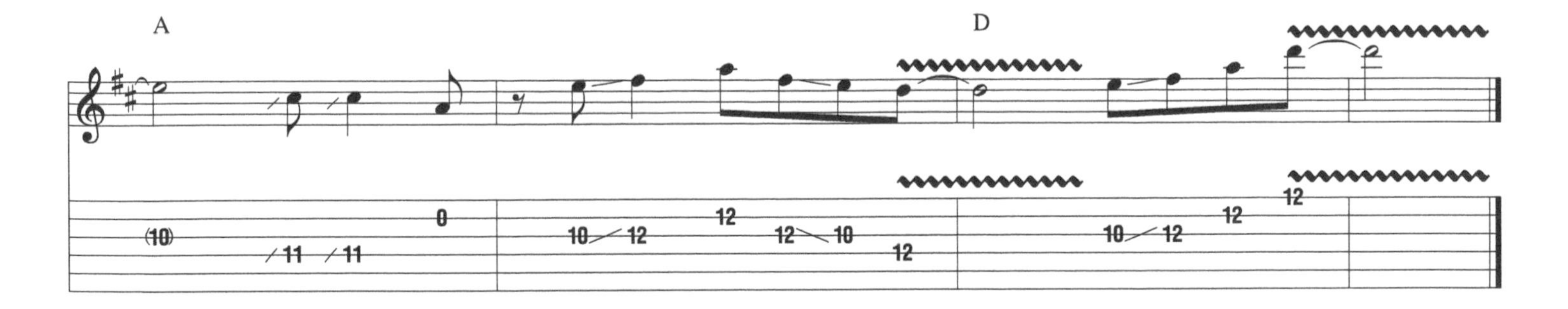

▶ ***Use the scales in other places to play in keys other than D while in D tuning.*** The following version of "Twelve O'Clock" is in the key of C, so the ad-lib solo is based on the 12th fret blues box moved down to the 10th fret, because C is at the 10th fret/barre.

Twelve O'Clock (in C)

D Tuning

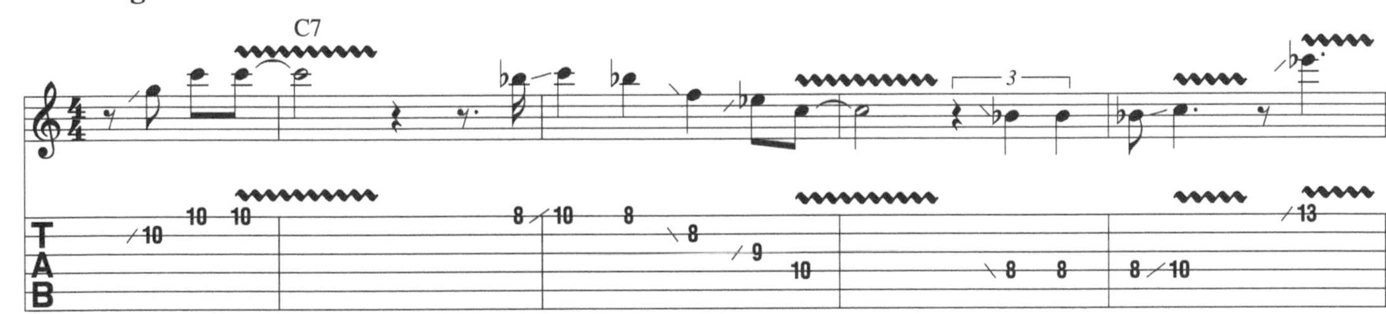

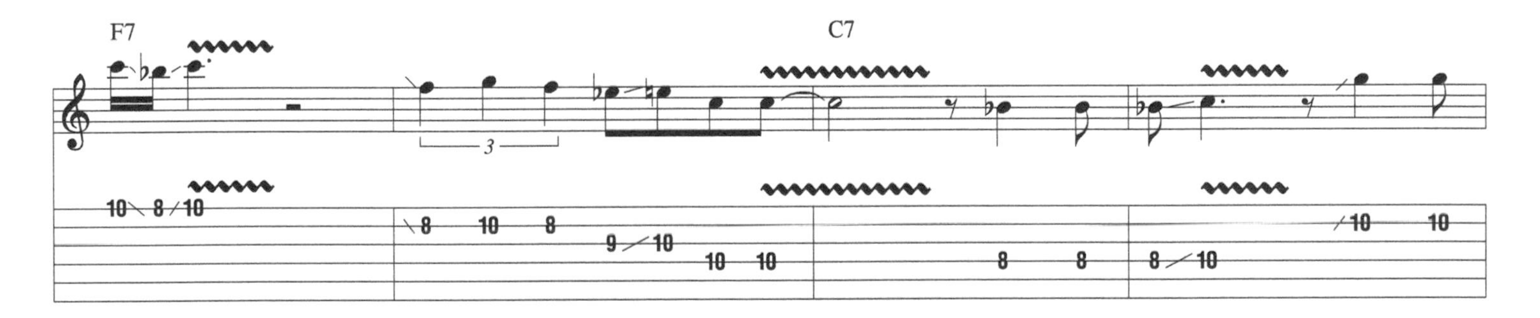

SUMMING UP—NOW YOU KNOW...

- ▶ *How to play a D blues scale at the 12th fret.*
- ▶ *How to play a D major scale at the 12th fret.*
- ▶ *How to use both scales to play melodies, and ad lib solos and licks.*
- ▶ *How use the scales to play in keys other than D, while in D tuning*

#6 D TUNING: BARRED CHORDS

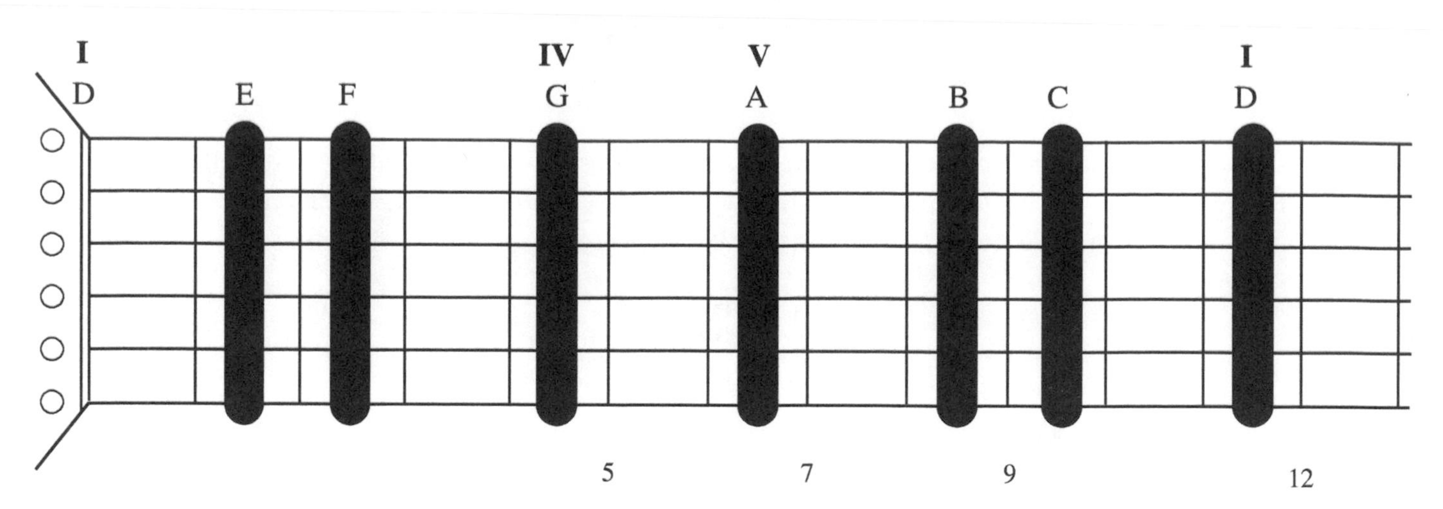

WHY?

► In D tuning, just as in G tuning, you can base solos and backup on barred chords.

WHAT?

► **ROADMAP #6** ***shows the barred chords in D tuning.***

► ***Barre the indicated major chords with a slide or your index finger.***

► ***The fretboard "starts over" at the 12th fret.*** The D barre at the 12th fret matches the open string D chord; the 14th fret/E chord matches the 2nd fret/E, and so on.

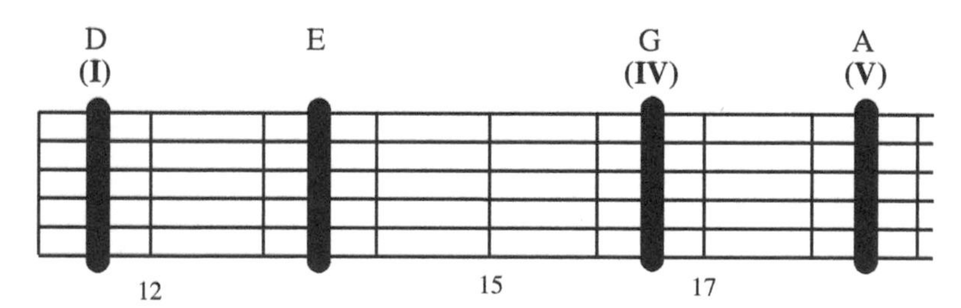

HOW?

► ***You can play chord-based licks and melodies by following a song's chord changes,*** playing the appropriate barred chords.

► ***Play the barred notes and the blues or major scale notes*** described in **ROADMAP #5**:

F barre chord with blues scale notes

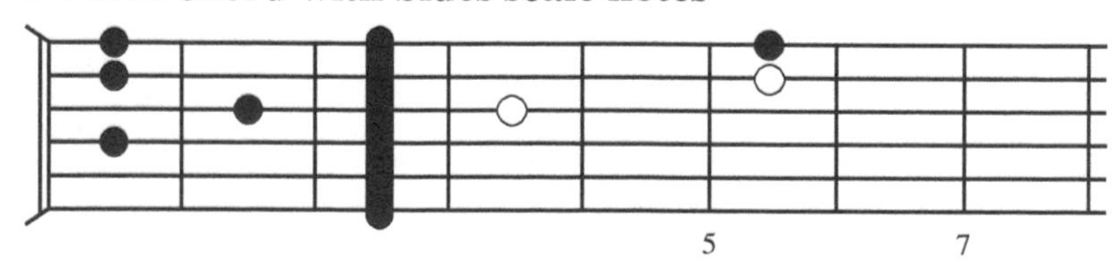

F barre chord with major scale notes

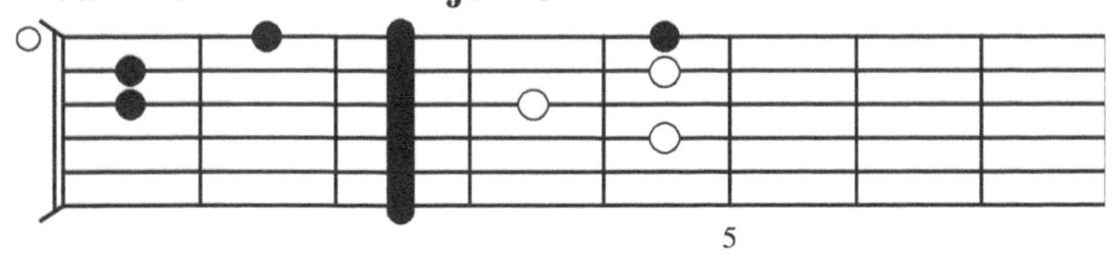

▶ ***The 2nd and 3rd strings (or just the 2nd string), three frets above a barre, make a 7th chord:***

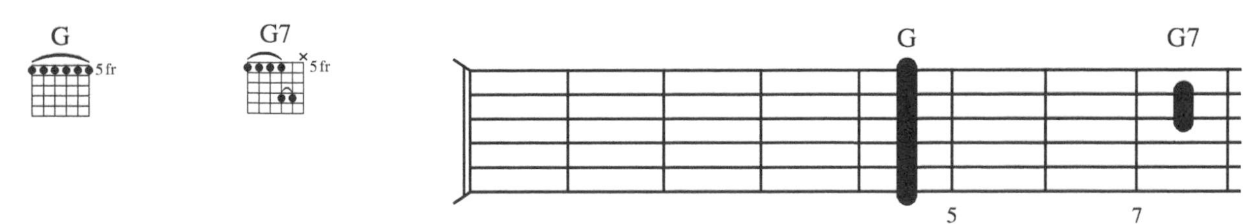

▶ ***You can locate minor chords by relating them to barre chords, as shown in the chart below, which indicates A minor chords:***

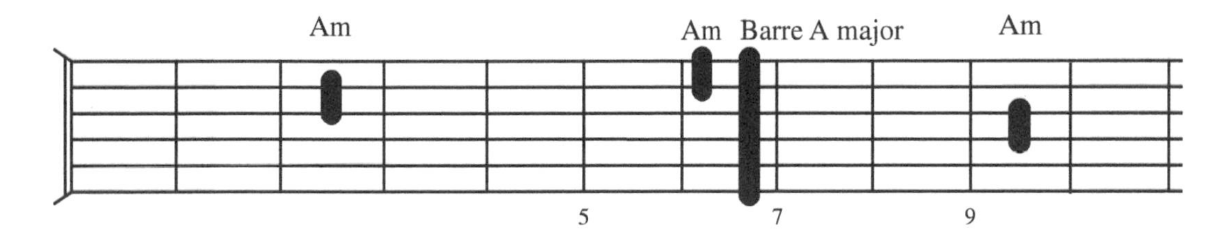

▶ There's a minor chord on the 1st and 2nd strings, at the barre.

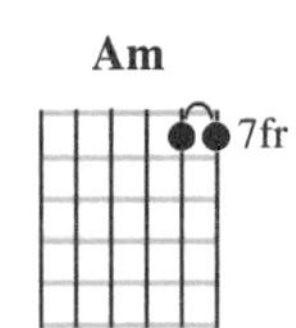

▶ There's a minor chord on the 2nd and 3rd strings, four frets below the barre.

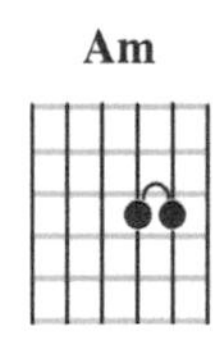

▶ There's a minor chord on the 3rd and 4th strings, three frets above the barre.

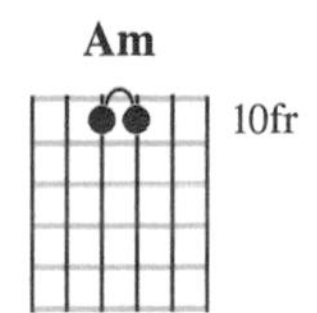

DO IT!

▶ ***Play the melody to "Careless Love" by barring the song's chords.*** Notice the use of 7th chords in the fills, during pauses in the melody line.

Careless Love II (with Barred Chords)

▶ ***The following instrumental, "Dimestore," has a very popular chord progression that includes a few minor chords.***

Dimestore

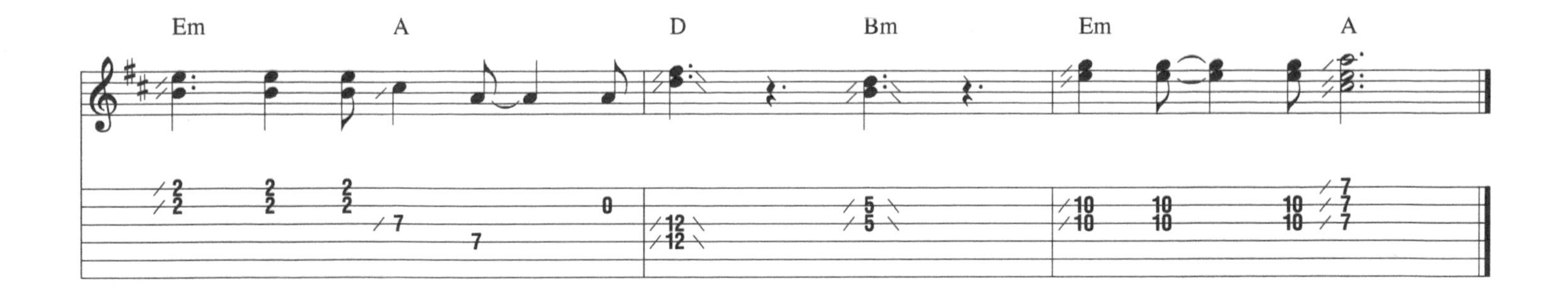

▶ ***You can play chord-based solos in other keys, while tuned to open D***, by using the licks and ideas in the last several tunes. The following key-of-E version of "Stagolee" is a good example:

Stagolee II

SUMMING UP—NOW YOU KNOW…

- ▶ ***How to play all the barred major chords in D tuning.***
- ▶ ***How to make the barred major chords into 7ths.***
- ▶ ***How to make the barred major chords into minors.***
- ▶ ***How to play chord-based solos and backup in D tuning.***
- ▶ ***How to play chord-based solos and backup in keys other than D, using D tuning.***

THE G/A AND D/E CONVERSION

G Tuning - Blues Scale

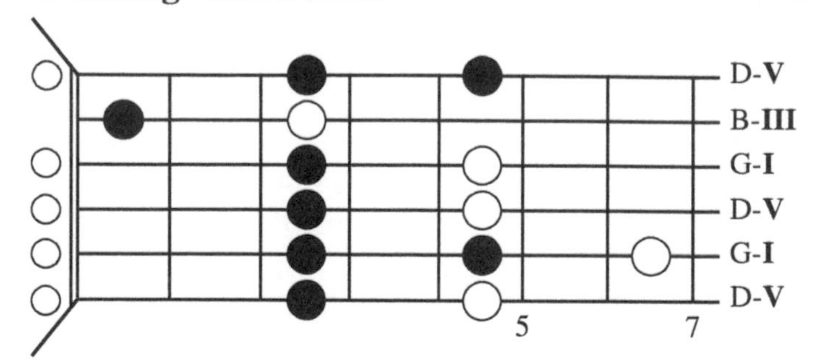

D Tuning - Blues Scale

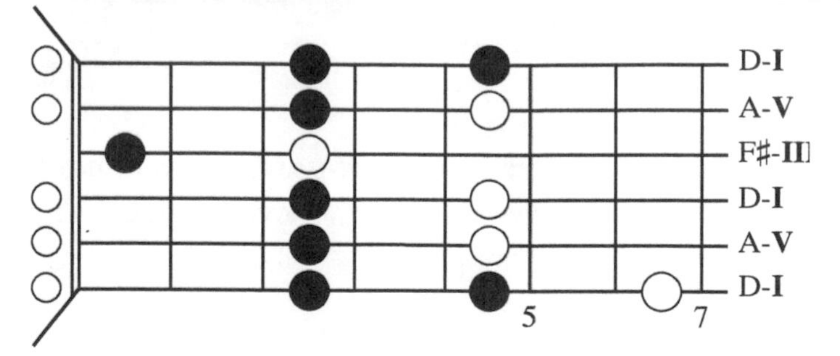

A Tuning - Blues Scale

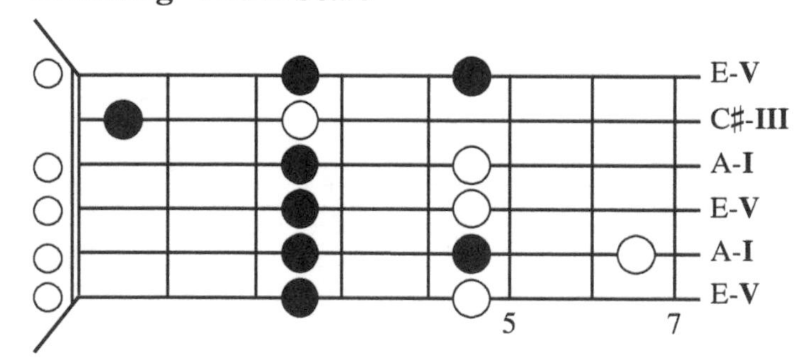

E Tuning - Blues Scale

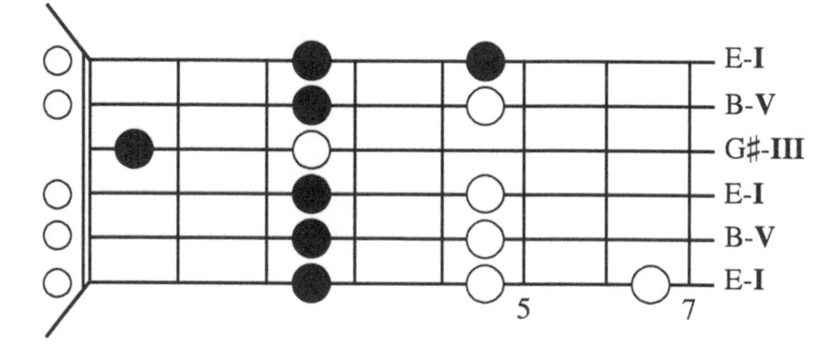

WHY?

- Open A and open E are popular tunings among slide guitarists. You can automatically play in these tunings if you understand their relationship to open G and open D.

WHAT?

- ***Open A tuning is the same as open G, but every string is tuned two frets higher.*** Robert Johnson played many of his slide songs in this tuning.
- ***In A tuning, you can play all the G tuning licks, scales, chords and solos.***
- ***Open E tuning is the same as open D, but every string is tuned two frets higher***. It was Duane Allman's favorite slide tuning.
- ***In E tuning, you can play all the D tuning licks, scales, chords and solos.***

HOW?

- ***To get to A tuning from G tuning, tune every note up two frets.***
- ***To get to A tuning from standard tuning:***
  - Leave the 6th/E, 5th/A and 1st/E strings as they are.
  - Tune the 4th/D string up two frets, to E. Match it to the open 6th string.
  - Tune the 3rd/G string up two frets, to A. Match it to the open 5th string.
  - Tune the 2nd/B up two fret, to C♯. Match it to the 3rd string/4th fret.

- ▶ ***To get to E tuning from D tuning, tune every note up two frets.***
- ▶ ***To get to E tuning from standard tuning:***
  - ▷ Leave the 6th/E, 2nd/B and 1st/E strings as they are.
  - ▷ Tune the 5th/A string up two frets, to B. Match it to the open 2nd string.
  - ▷ Tune the 4th/D string up two frets, to E. Match it to the open 6th string.
  - ▷ Tune the 3rd/G string up one fret, to G♯. Match it to the 4th string/4th fret.
- ▶ ***When you play open G-style solos or licks in A tuning, they are in the key of A,*** and the names of chords and notes move up two frets. The G blues scale is an A blues scale; a barre at the 5th fret is D instead of C, and so on.
- ▶ ***The same goes for playing open D-style solos or licks in E tuning.*** The names of notes and chords move up two frets to the key of E.

DO IT!

- ▶ ***Play a solo in E tuning, using D scales and chords.*** The following rock solo features first position and 12th fret soloing and chord-based licks.

Rockin' E

E Tuning

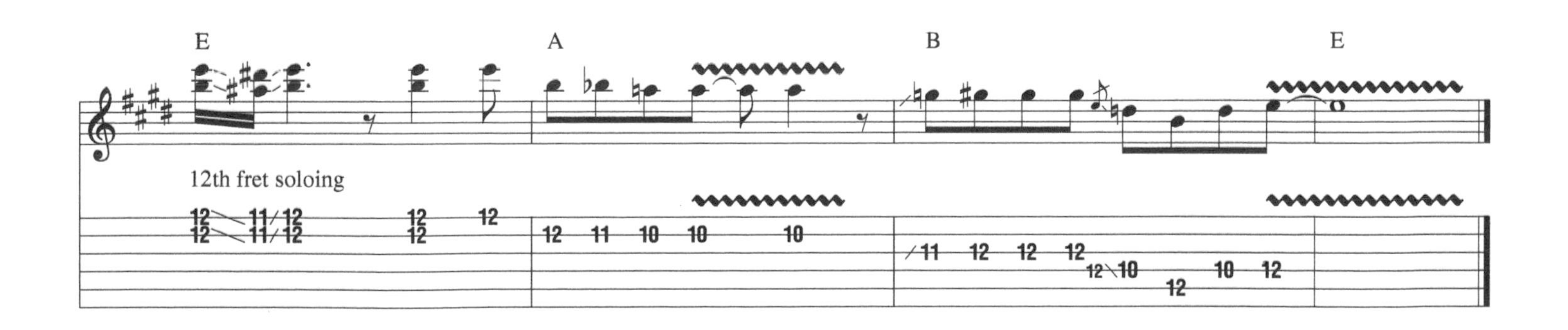

▶ ***Play a solo in A tuning, using G scales and chords.*** The 12-bar blues that follows makes use of all the G soloing ideas of **ROADMAPS #1**, **#2** and **#3**.

A Solo

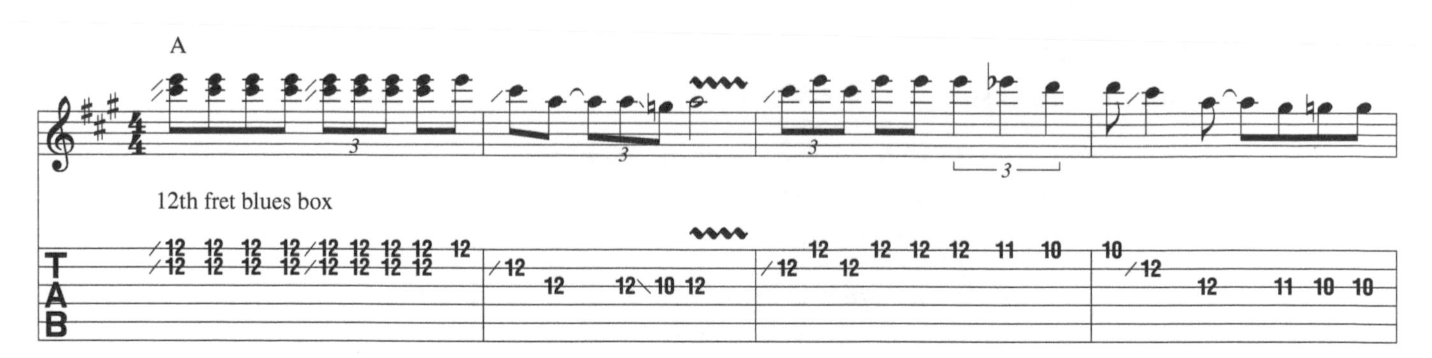

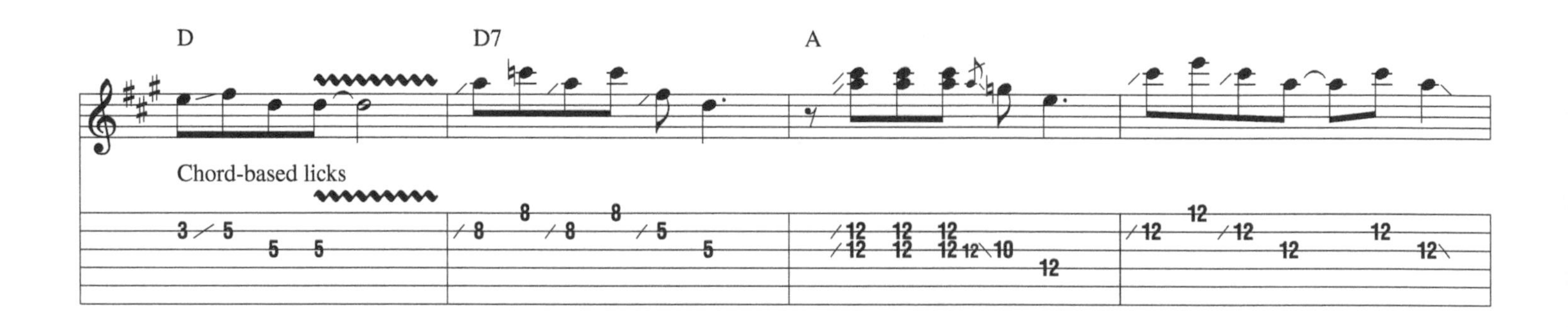

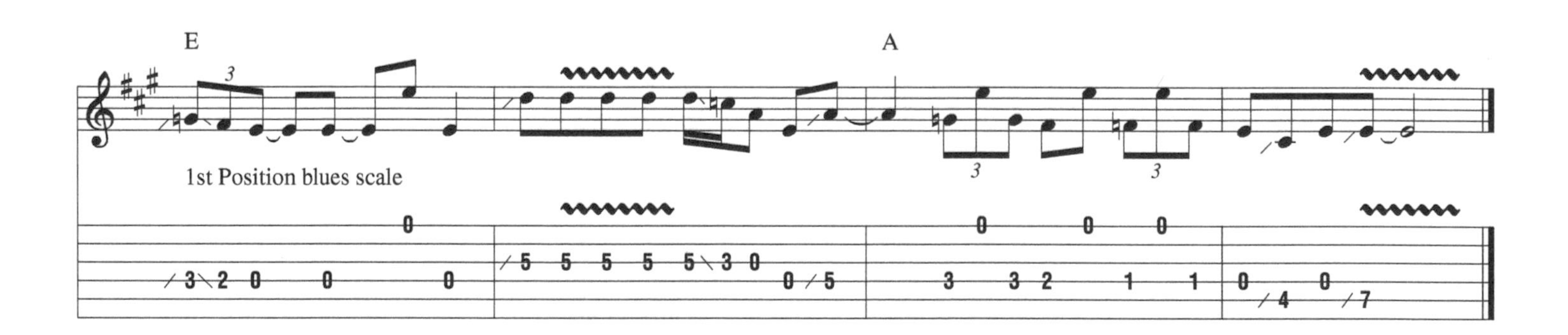

SUMMING UP—NOW YOU KNOW…

▶ ***How to play in A tuning.***

▶ ***How to play in E tuning.***

#8 THE G/D CONVERSION

G Tuning

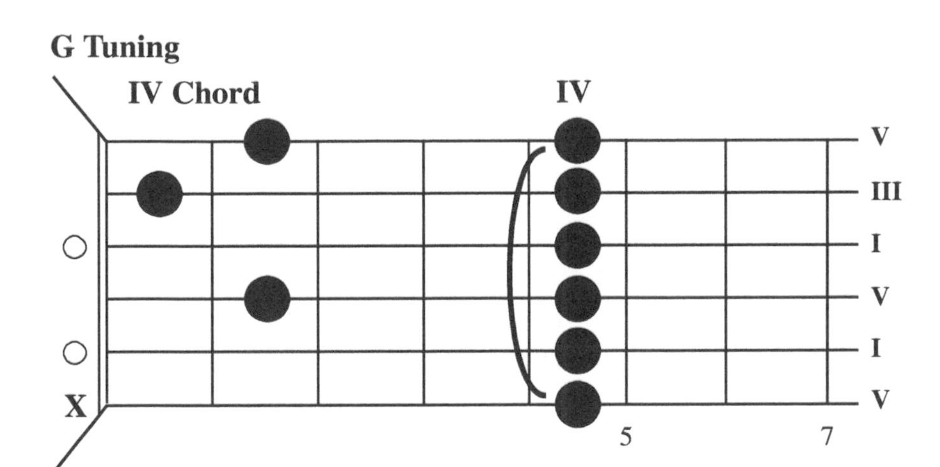

D Tuning

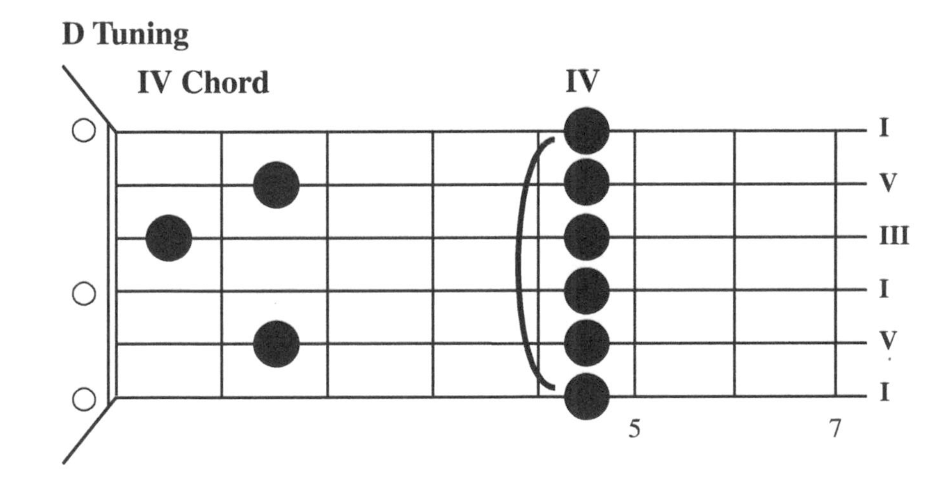

Both Tunings

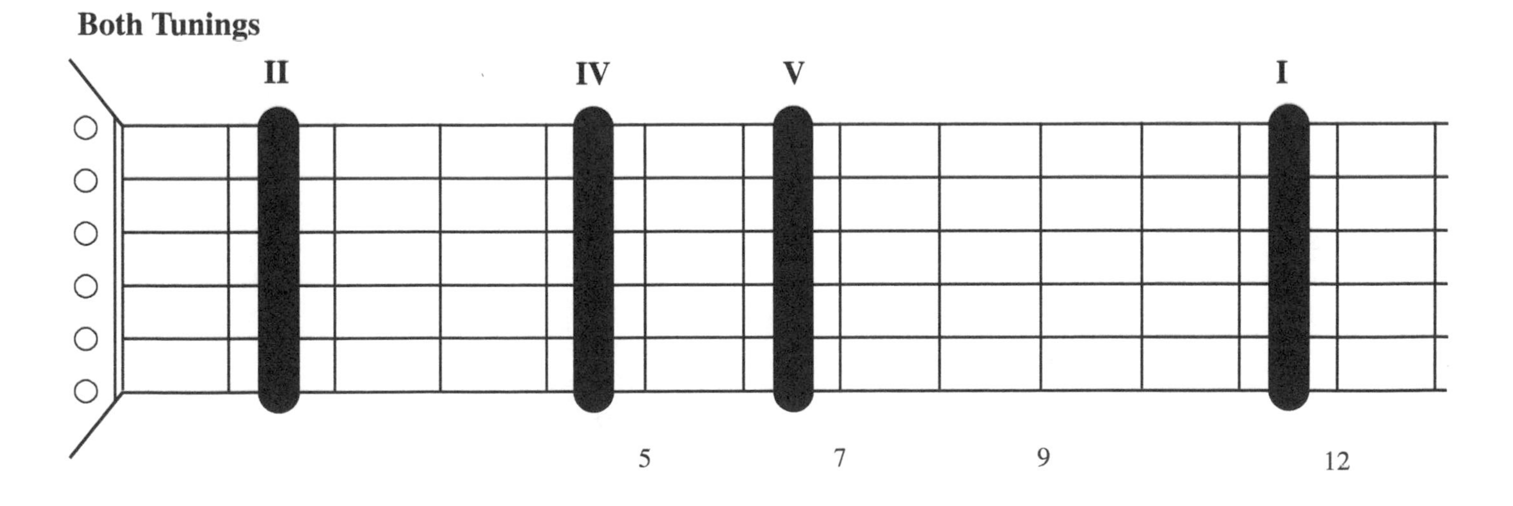

WHY?

- ▶ There's a relationship between the G and D tunings that makes it possible for you to borrow licks or solos from one tuning and use them in the other.

WHAT?

- ***In both tunings, barred chords have the same interval relationships on the fretboard.*** In both tunings, the I chord is open and at the 12th fret; the IV chord is at the 5th fret; the V chord is at the 7th fret, and so on (II chord at the 2nd fret; III chord at the 4th fret).*

- ***In D tuning, you can use G licks, scales, solos and chords if you "move them up a string."*** A G tuning lick that is played on the 1st and 2nd strings can be played in D tuning on the 2nd and 3rd strings. That's because the G tuning/string-to-string intervals on the top five strings (1st, 2nd, 3rd, 4th and 5th) match the D tuning/string-to-string intervals on the bottom five strings (2nd, 3rd, 4th, 5th and 6th).

Moving the IV chord up a string

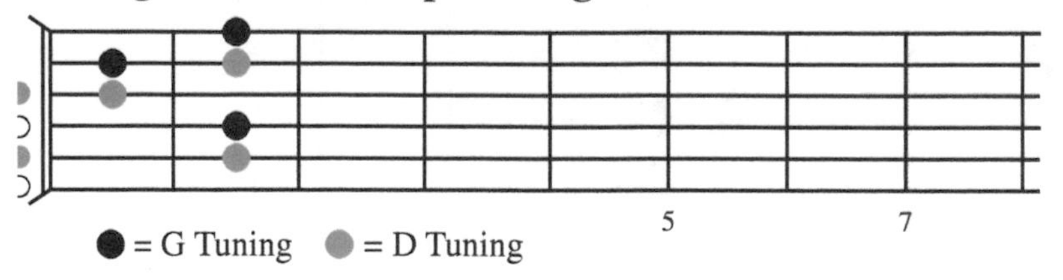

- ***Similarly, you can steal many D tuning licks, scales, solos and chords and use them in G tuning by "moving them down a string."*** Any D tuning lick or chord that doesn't use the 1st string is eligible for this conversion.

HOW?

- ***When in D tuning, play a G lick by pretending the 2nd string/A is the 1st string and the real 1st string/D is missing.*** Here are some G tuning turnarounds converted to D tuning. Note that chords, as well as licks, are "moved up a string." (A *turnaround* is a lick that ends an 8- or 12-bar phrase in a blues tune.)

29

G Tuning

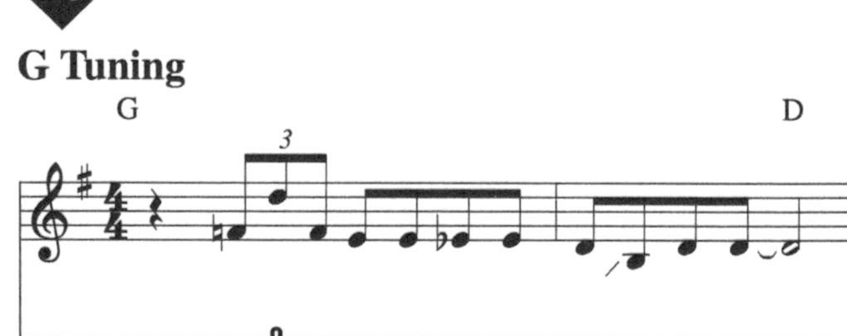

D Tuning

G Tuning

D Tuning

▶ ***When in G tuning, play a D tuning lick by moving it up a string.*** A D-tuning lick on the 6th and 5th strings translates over to G tuning on the 5th and 4th strings, as this boogie lick on the bass strings illustrates:

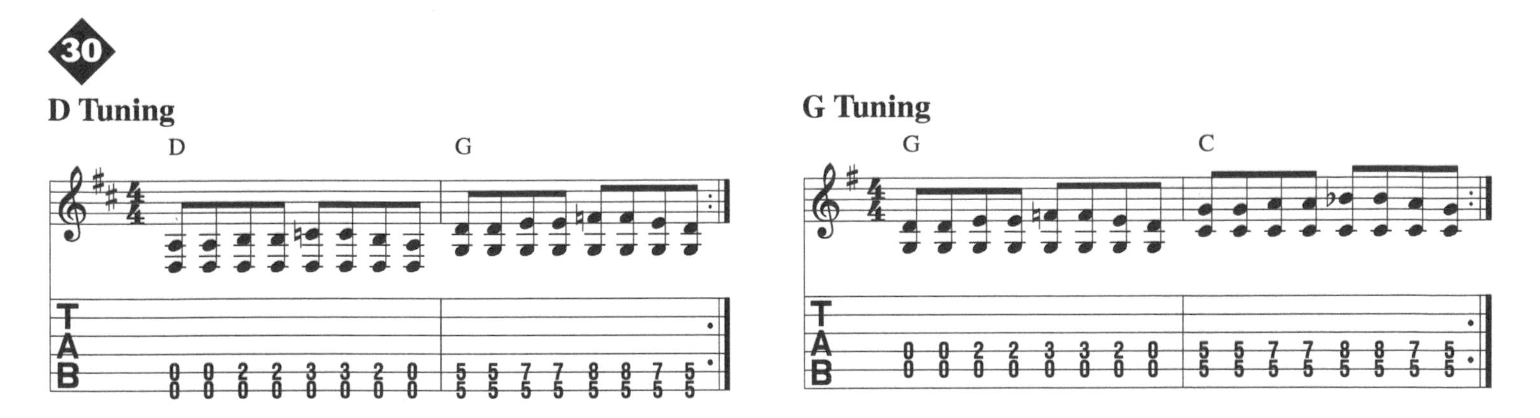

DO IT!

▶ ***Here's "Chilly Winds" in D tuning, transposed from the G tuning version in the* ROADMAP #1 *chapter.*** It's the exact same solo as in that chapter, moved up a string.

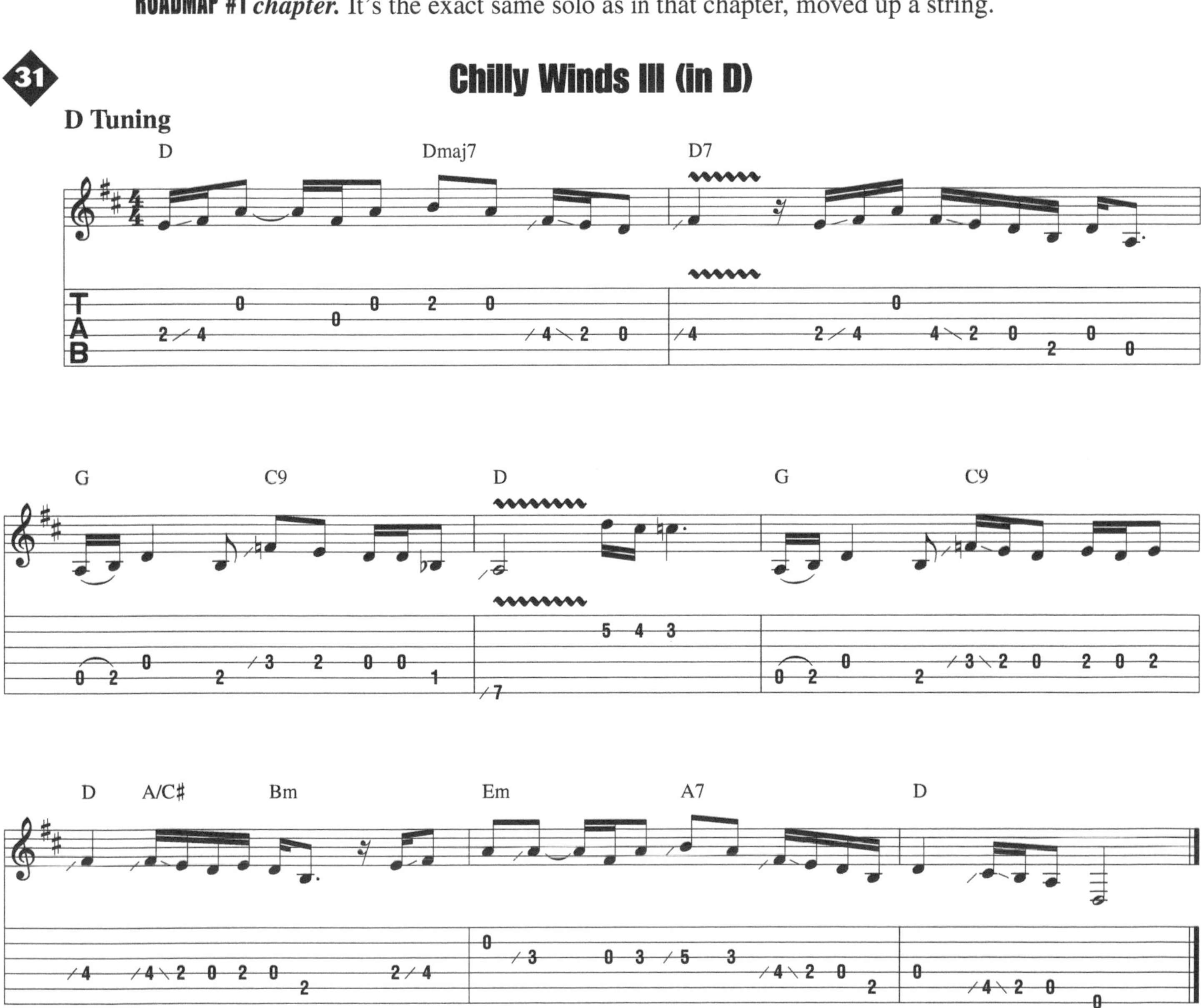

▶ ***Here's "Careless Love," in G tuning, transposed from the D tuning version in the* ROADMAP #6 *chapter.*** It's moved down a string from the G arrangement, and two or three notes were changed to accommodate D tuning.

Careless Love III (in G)

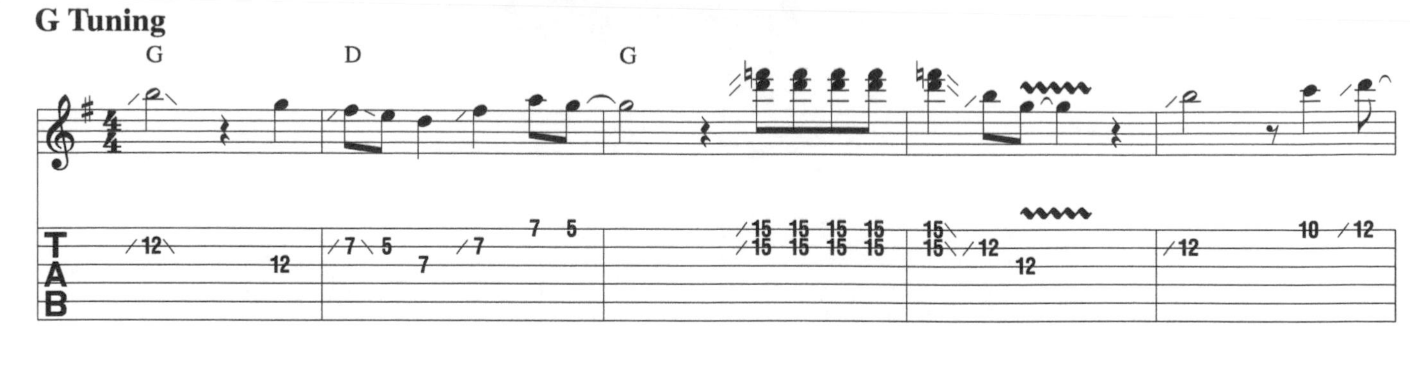

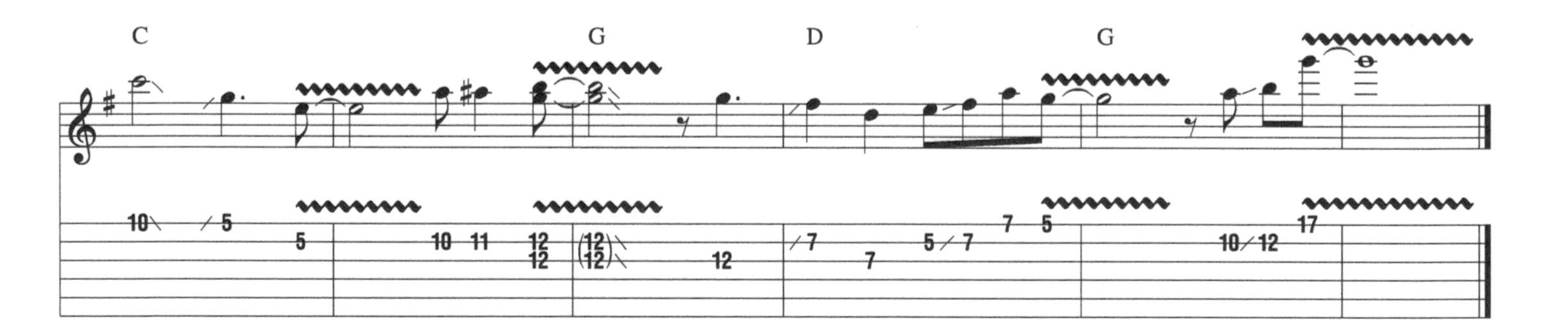

SUMMING UP—NOW YOU KNOW…

▶ ***How to convert G tuning licks, solos or chords to D tuning.***

▶ ***How to convert D tuning licks, solos or chords to G tuning.***

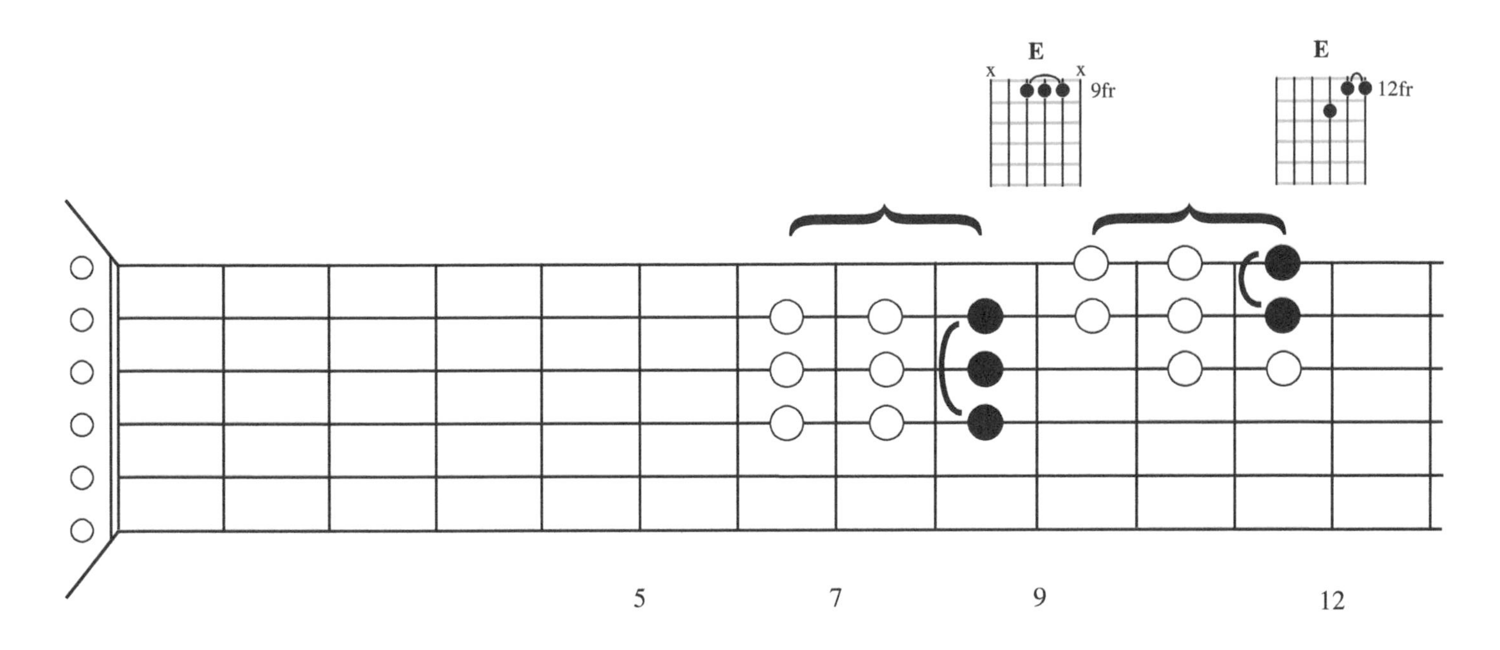

WHY?

- Muddy Waters, Robert Nighthawk, Earl Hooker and other blues slidemasters popularized standard tuning slide in the key of E. (E is a convenient key for slide in standard tuning because of the E and A bass strings.) Playing slide in standard tuning saves the performing musician from the bother of retuning to play slide, and tuning back to standard for non-slide numbers.

WHAT?

- ***The black dots on Fretboard #9 are partial E chords.*** They are notes you can play when an E chord is played in a tune.
- ***In a bluesy tune in the key of E, these notes can be played throughout all the chord changes.***
- ***The white circles on the fretboards above are "passing tones."*** Along with the black dots, they create little blues boxes, or scale positions.

HOW?

- ***The black dots relate to the indicated E chord shapes.***

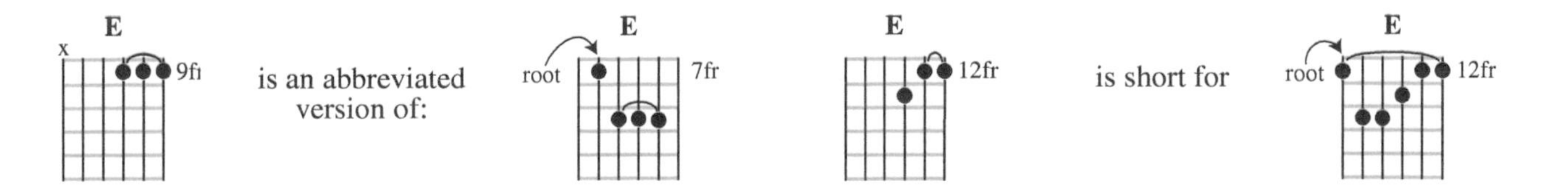

- ***During an E chord, you seldom pause (end a lick) on a passing tone.*** But some passing tones will work as phrase-ending notes with the A and B chords. Experiment!

▶ ***Here are some E licks based on the blues boxes of* ROADMAP #9:**

33

▶ ***For variety, you can re-create the E blues box pattern for A and B chords.***

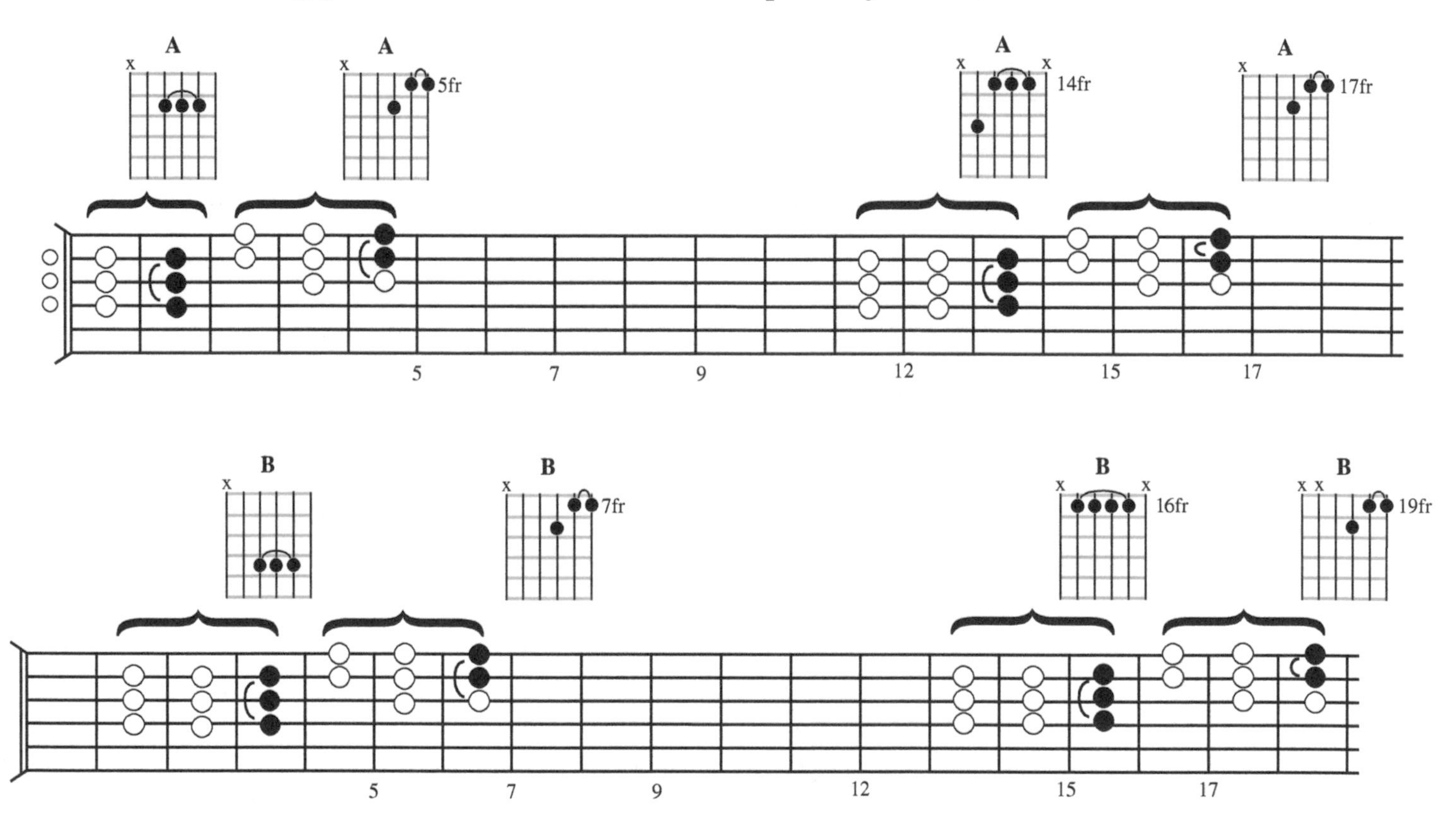

▶ ***Here are some A and B licks based on the blues boxes above:***

34

DO IT!

▶ ***Play the following 8-bar blues using just the E blues boxes:***

8-Bar Blues

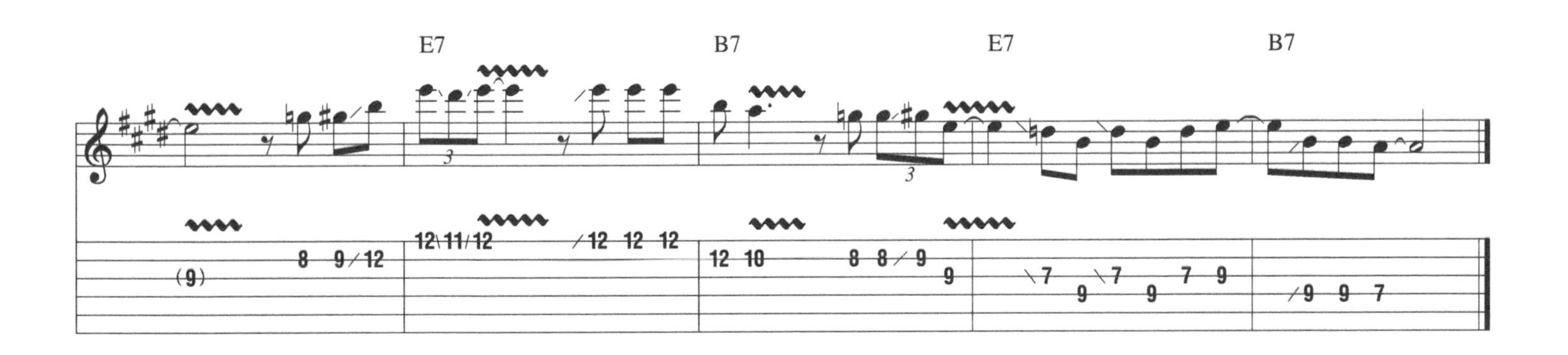

▶ ***Play the same 8-bar blues using E, A and B blues boxes:***

8-Bar Blues II (with Three Blues Boxes)

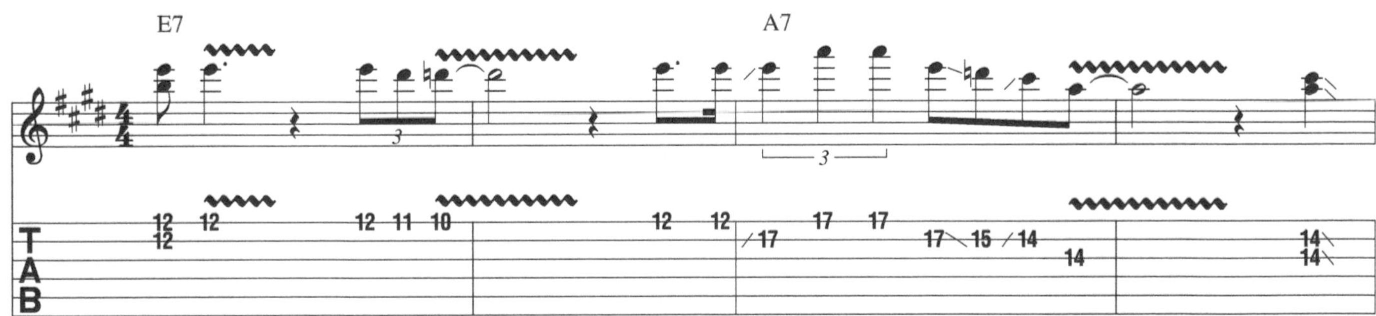

▶ *This 12-bar blues mixes all the blues boxes in typical Muddy Waters fashion:*

SUMMING UP—NOW YOU KNOW….

- ▶ *How to play slide in standard tuning on bluesy songs in E.*
- ▶ *Several blues boxes that are useful for slide in standard tuning.*

#10 STANDARD TUNING, ANY KEY

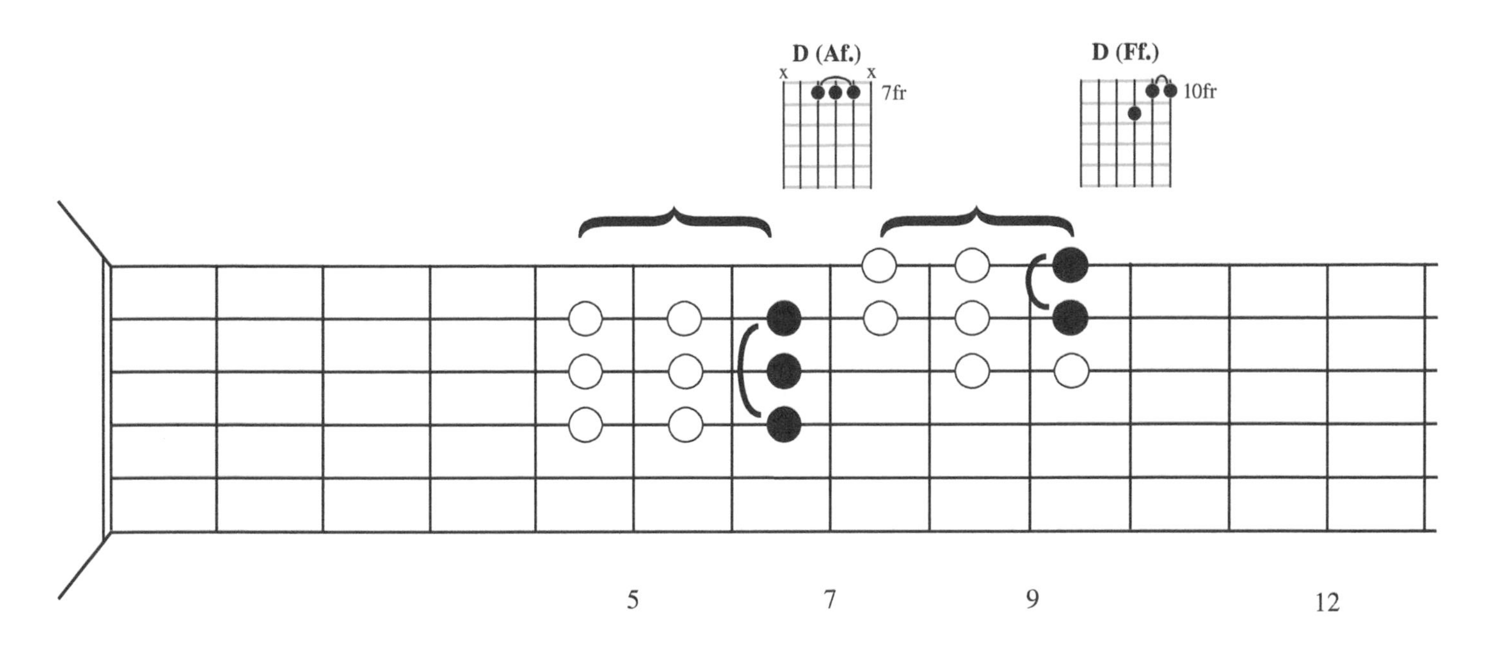

WHY?

- **ROADMAP #9** can be altered to make it possible to play slide in standard tuning in any key. This method makes re-tuning unnecessary.

WHAT?

- ***In* ROADMAP #10*, the black dots are partial D chords.***
- ***The circles are passing tones. Together with the black dots, they are blues boxes for the key of D.***
- ***In a bluesy tune in the key of D, these blues boxes can be played throughout all the chord changes.***

HOW?

- ***The black dots relate to the indicated D chord shapes.*** The chord shapes are labeled Af. (A formation) and Ff. (F formation):

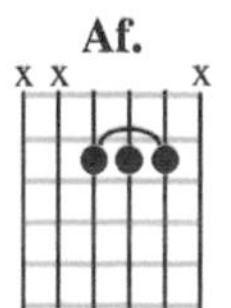

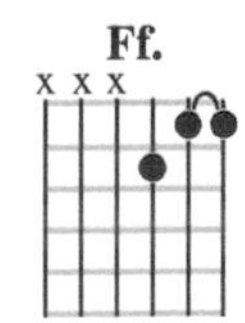

▶ You can create a similar roadmap for any chord, making blues boxes out of the partial A and F formations. For example, here's the roadmap for a C chord:

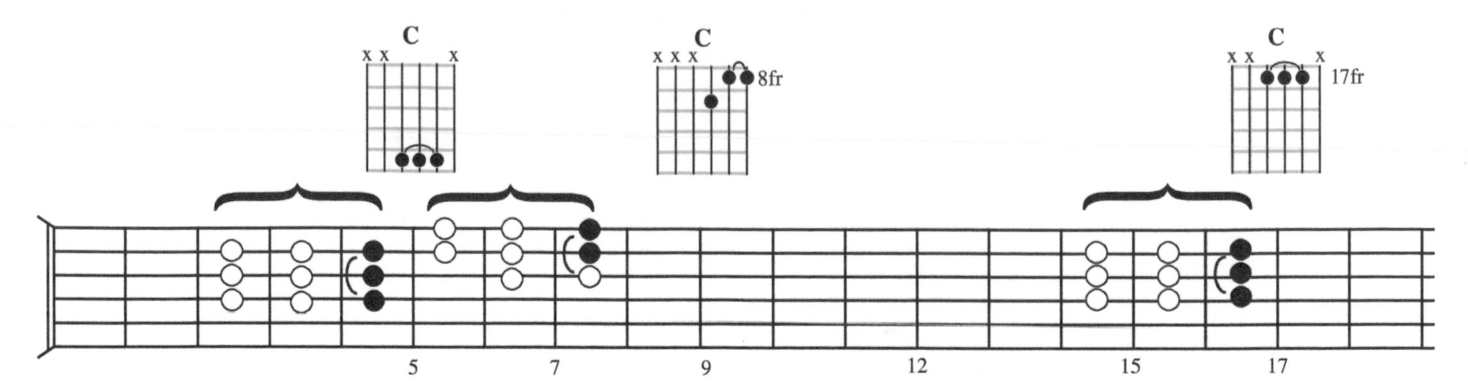

DO IT!

▶ ***Play the "8-Bar Blues" from* ROADMAP # 9 *(the first version, page 39), but transpose it to the key of C:****

38

8-Bar Blues III (Key of C)

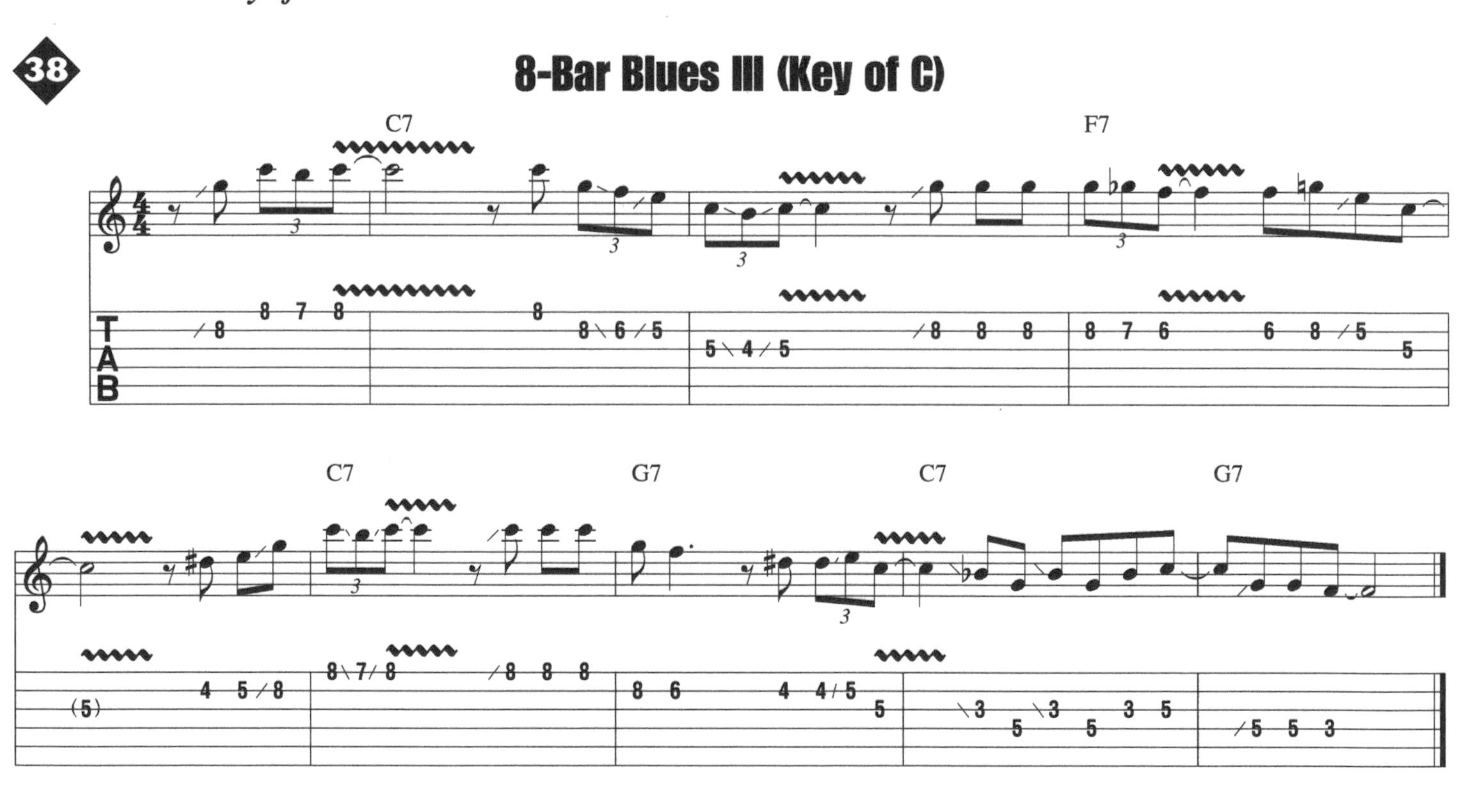

▶ ***Play "8-Bar Blues II"* (ROADMAP #9) *in the key of D.* ROADMAP #10** shows the blues boxes for D; here are the G and A roadmaps:

G Boxes

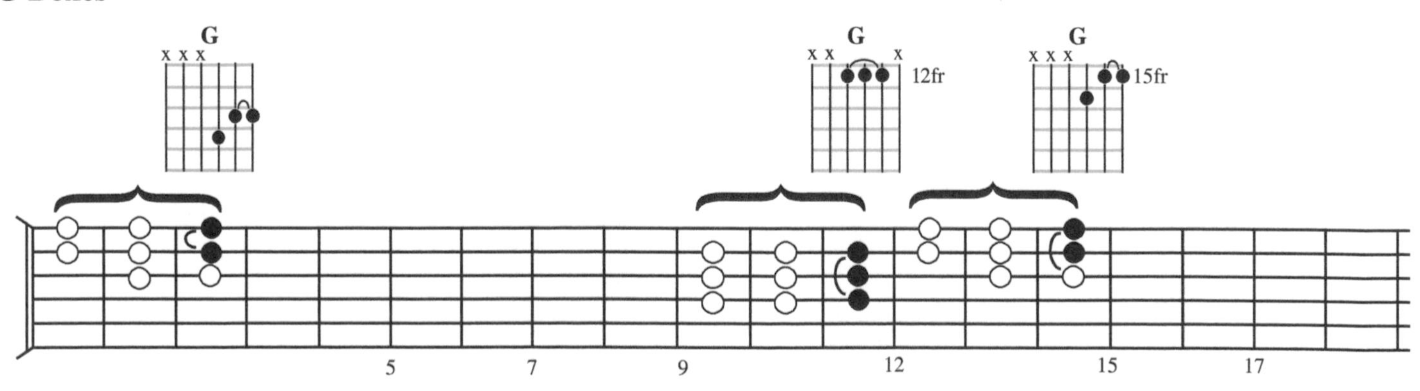

* To "transpose" is to play a piece of music in a different key than it was originally played or written.

A Boxes

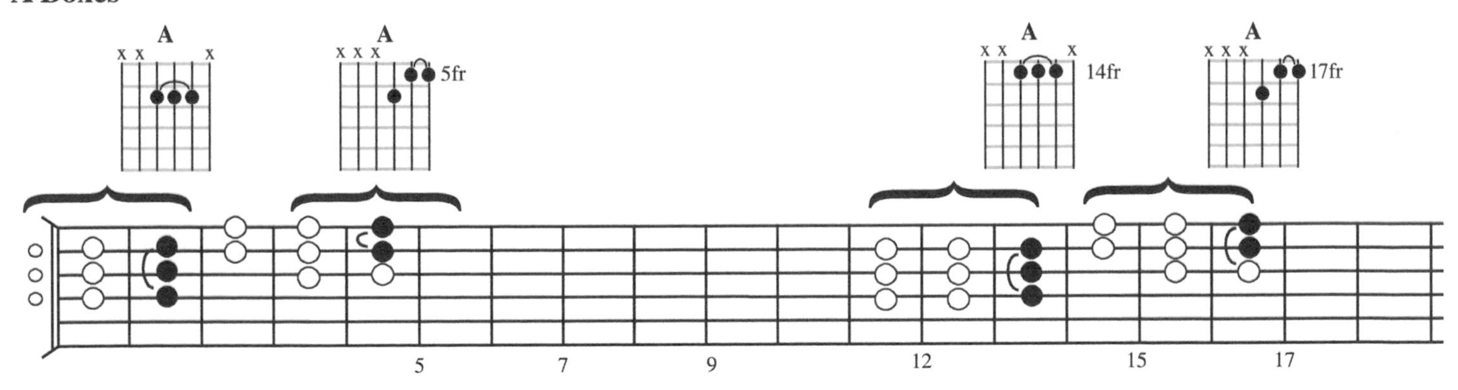

8-Bar Blues IV (Key of D)

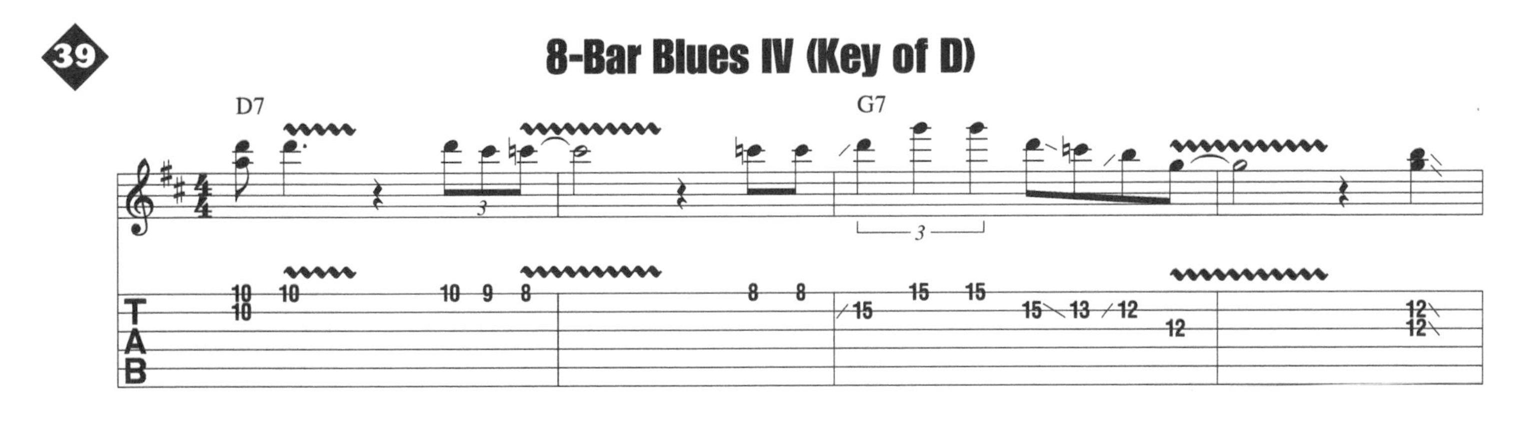

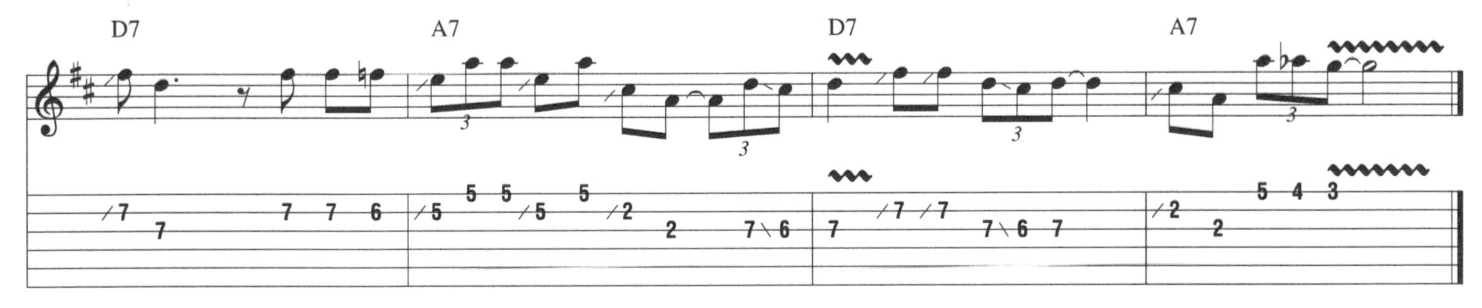

SUMMING UP—NOW YOU KNOW…

- ▶ *How to transpose the positions of* **ROADMAP #9** *to other keys.*
- ▶ *How to play slide in any key, in standard tuning.*

STANDARD TUNING: BLUES BOXES

A Blues Boxes

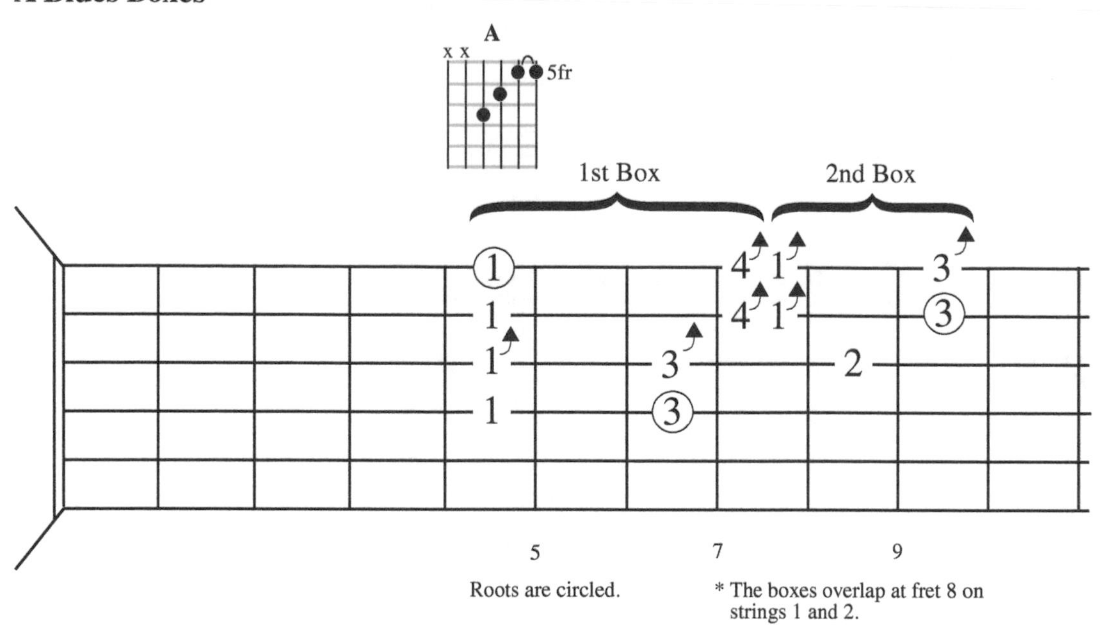

WHY?

- Slide can enhance the standard blues boxes that guitarists like B.B. King, Eric Clapton, and most contemporary blues and rock players use.

WHAT?

- **ROADMAP #11** ***shows the first two blues boxes for the key of A.*** The numbers are fingering suggestions.
- ***The notes of both boxes can be played in a bluesy tune, throughout the chord changes.***
- ***The notes with arrows (4↑, 1↑) can be stretched or choked.***
- ***Players who enhance the blues boxes with slide, switch back and forth from fretted notes to "slide notes."*** The notes with stretch indications are particularly good for sliding.

HOW?

- ***Get your left hand in position for the first blues box by fingering the appropriate F formation.*** For an A blues box, play a 5th fret/F formation. It's an A chord:

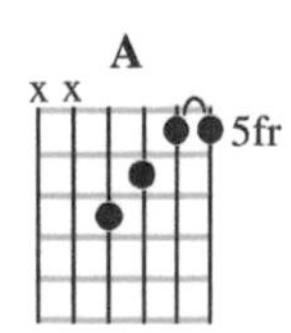

- ***You can slide up to any note in the boxes.***

▶ *Instead of stretching the indicated strings, you can slide up one or two frets:*

40

Stretching strings **Sliding the same strings**

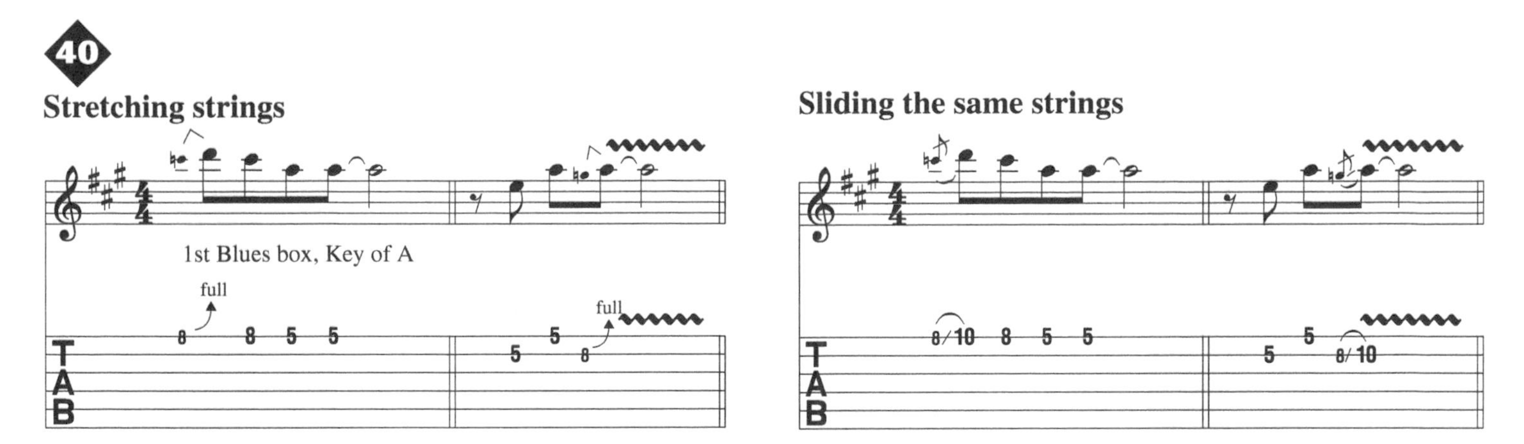

▶ *Here are some typical blues box licks in A, enhanced by slides:*

41

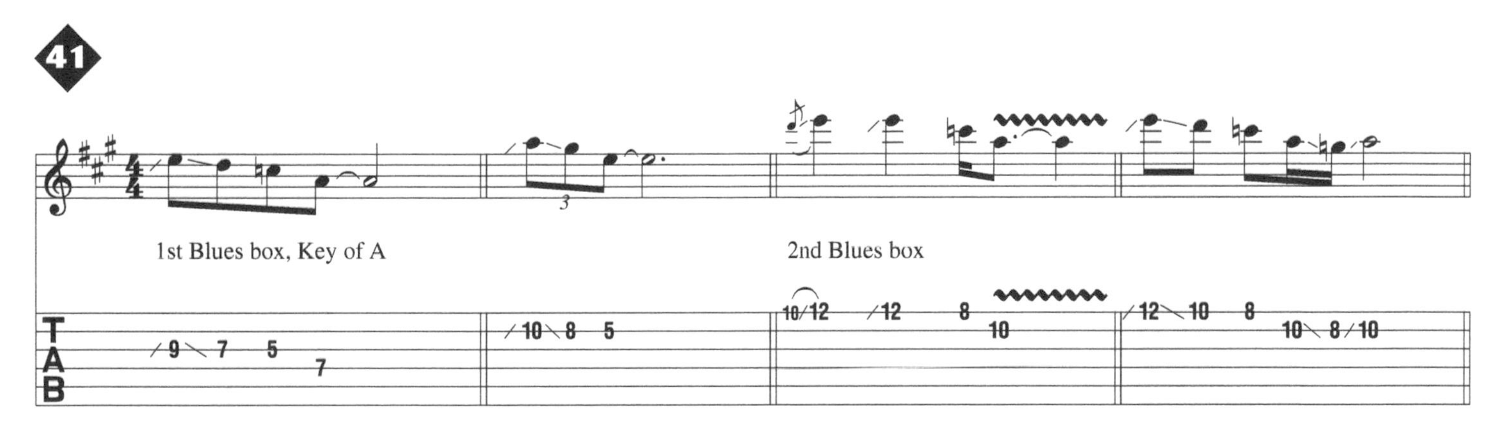

DO IT!

▶ *Practice 1st and 2nd blues box/slide licks with this R&B tune in the key of A:*

42

▶ ***This blues shuffle is in C, so play the F formation at the 8th fret*** to be "in position" for the first blues box:

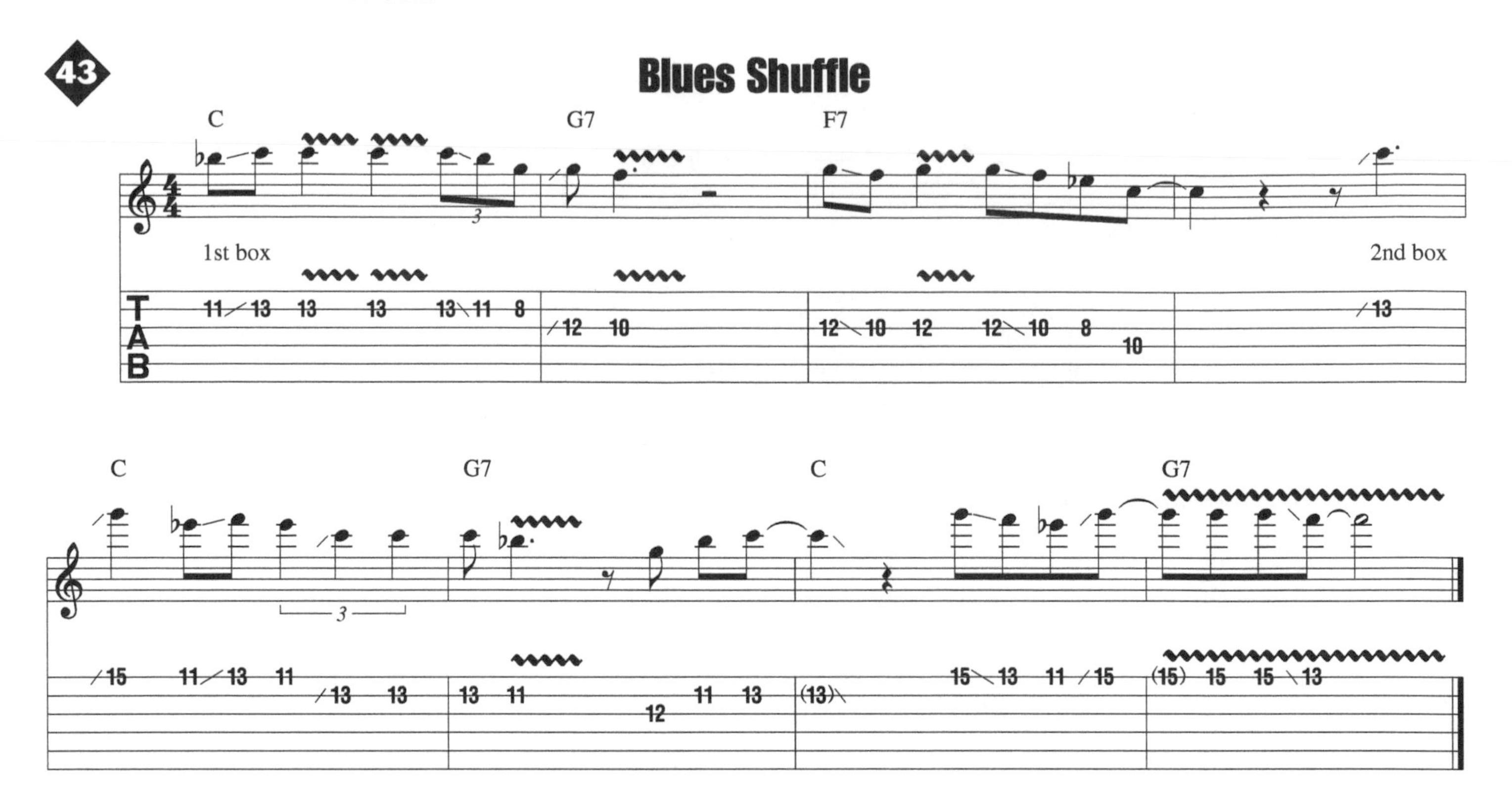

SUMMING UP—NOW YOU KNOW…

▶ ***How to use the first and second blues box to solo in bluesy tunes, in any key.***

▶ ***How to enhance those licks with a slide.***

#12 REVISUALIZING ROADMAPS WITH THE CAPO

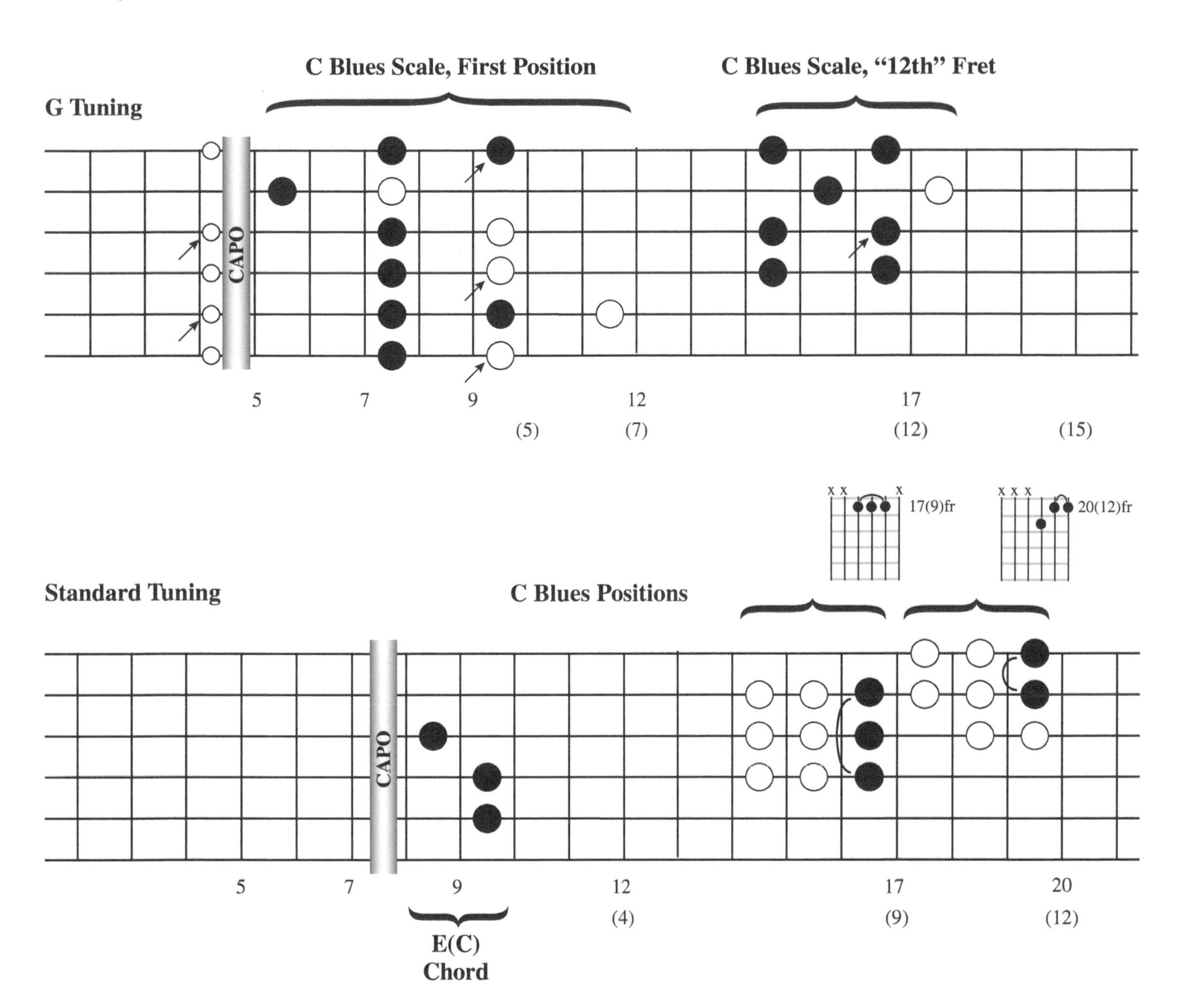

WHY?

- ▶ The capo gives you more choices with respect to key.
  - ▷ Robert Johnson had a high voice and liked to sing in B, so he often played in open A tuning and capoed up two frets.
  - ▷ Muddy Waters favored standard tuning/E licks, as in **ROADMAP #9**, but some songs were too low for his voice in the key of E. He capoed as far up as the 8th fret to suit his voice and still play those E slide licks.
  - ▷ Playing music with other people, you may be asked to jam in any key (E♭, F, C, C♯, etc.) because of someone else's vocal or instrumental needs. Using a capo, you can choose an open or standard tuning, depending on what sound or style of slide playing you prefer.

▷ Different tunings have different *moods,* so it's good to have several options for any tune: you may want the dark sound of open G, the warmer sound of open D, and so on.

WHAT?

- ***The diagrams above show two ways to play in the key of C:***
  - ▷ In G tuning, capoed at the 5th fret
  - ▷ In standard tuning, capoed at the 8th fret (for playing E licks)
- Each diagram shows the positions or boxes for slide in C. The frets in parenthesis are in respect to the capo. In the G tuning roadmap, the fret called (5) is actually the 10th fret.
- ***Both diagrams duplicate other roadmaps "moved up several frets" by the capo.*** The G tuning diagram is **ROADMAPS #1** and **#2** combined and raised five frets. The standard tuning diagram is **#9**, eight frets higher.

HOW?

- ***To use a capo, revisualize roadmaps you already know, pretending the capo is the nut.*** For example, in open tunings (G or D), the IV chord is five frets above the nut, and the V chord is seven frets above the nut. If you're capoed up two frets in G tuning, to play in the key of A, the IV chord (D) is five frets above the capo, at the "actual" 7th fret. The V chord (E) is seven frets above the capo, at the "actual" 9th fret.

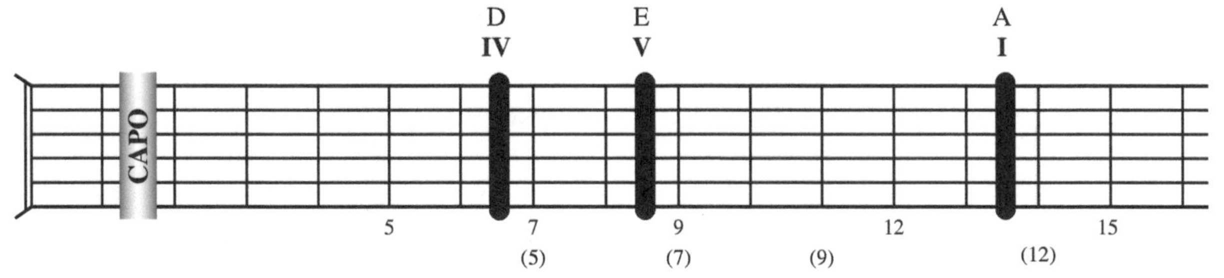

- ***To play in C using the G tuning roadmap:***
  - ▷ Capo up five frets, because a barre at the 5th fret is a C chord.
  - ▷ Pretend the 5th fret is the nut. Strum open strings and you'll hear a C chord.
  - ▷ The 6th fret is now the 1st fret, in respect to the capo.
  - ▷ Play G licks and solos, and they are all C licks.
- ***To play in C in standard tuning, using the Standard Tuning roadmap above:***
  - ▷ Capo up eight frets, because a barred E chord at the 8th fret is a C chord.
  - ▷ Pretend the 8th fret is the nut. Strum a first position E chord and it's a C.
  - ▷ Use the standard tuning playing positions eight frets higher than usual. The 12th fret position is now at the 20th fret.
- ***When you use a capo, use "actual names" of chords.***
  - ▷ If you're capoed at the 8th fret in standard tuning, an E chord is called "C," because a barred E at the 8th fret is actually a C chord, with or without a capo.
  - ▷ If you're capoed at the 4th fret in G tuning, to play in the key of B, strum across open strings and you'll hear a B chord, because, a barre at the 4th fret in G tuning is a B chord. The IV chord, E, is five frets up from the capo, at the "actual" 9th fret.

DO IT!

- ***Use the capo to play tunes you already know in G tuning.*** Play songs from the G tuning chapters, capoed up for other keys:

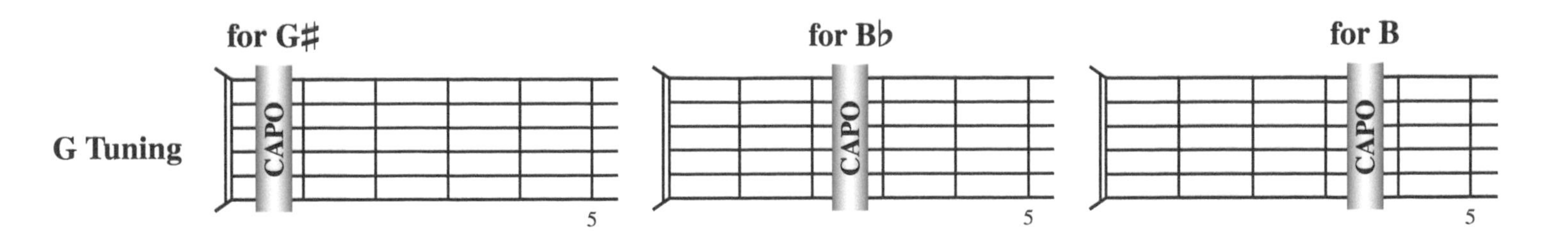

▶ *Do the same in D tuning:*

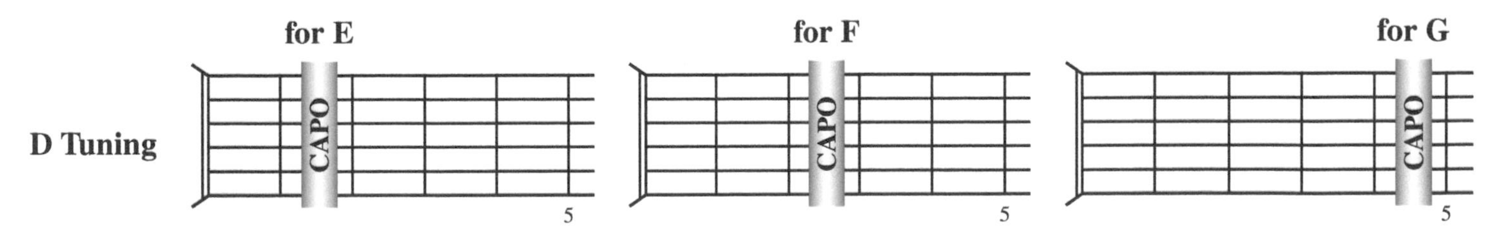

▶ ***Do the same in standard tuning, using the E licks*** as in **ROADMAP #9**.

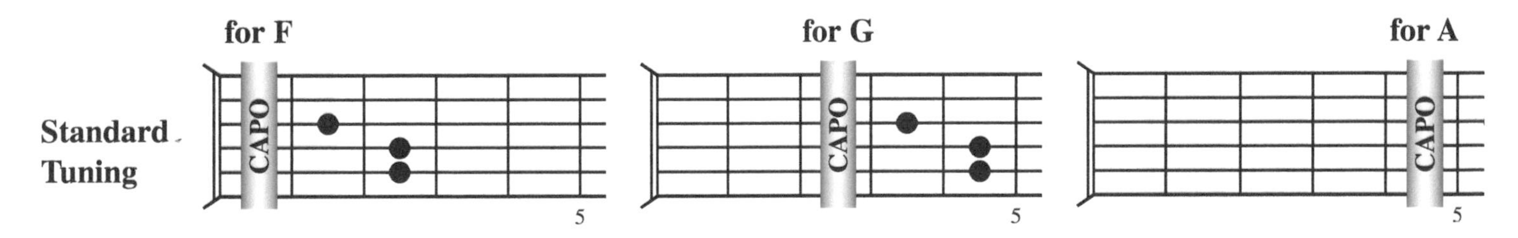

▶ The chart below gives you many capo options for every key. The first line gives you five ways to play in A: capoed up two frets in G tuning, tuned to open A with no capo, and so on.

Key	Open G	Open A	Open D	Open E	Standard	Other
A	capo 2	no capo	capo 7	capo 5	capo 5	—
B♭	capo 3	capo 1	capo 8	capo 6	capo 6	—
B	capo 4	capo 2	—	capo 7	capo 7	—
C	capo 5	capo 3	—	capo 8	capo 8	C tuning, (D tuning, 2 frets lower)
D♭	capo 6	capo 4	—	—	—	D♭ tuning, (D tuning, 1 fret lower)
D	capo 7	capo 5	no capo	—	—	—
E♭	capo 8	capo 6	capo 1	—	—	E♭ tuning, (D tuning, 1 fret higher)
E	—	capo 7	capo 2	no capo	no capo	—
F	—	capo 8	capo 3	capo 1	capo 1	F tuning, (G tuning, 2 frets lower)
G♭	—	—	capo 4	capo 2	capo 2	G♭ tuning, (G tuning, 1 fret lower)
G	no capo	—	capo 5	capo 3	capo 3	—
A♭	capo 1	—	capo 6	capo 4	capo 4	A♭ tuning, (G tuning, 1 fret higher)

SUMMING UP—NOW YOU KNOW…

▶ ***How to use a capo to play in many keys in G tuning.***

▶ ***How to use a capo to play in many keys in D tuning.***

▶ ***How to use a capo to play in many keys in standard tuning.***

USING THE PRACTICE TRACKS

On the five practice tracks, the lead guitar is separated from the rest of the band—it's on one side of your stereo. You can tune it out and use the band as backup, trying out any soloing techniques you like. You can also imitate the lead guitar; here are the soloing ideas on each track:

TRACK #1: R&B TUNE IN G
This one goes around the following 8-bar progression three times:

play 3 times

1	2	3	4	5	6	7	8
𝄆 G	𝄎	B♭	𝄎	C	C F	G	𝄎 𝄇

The lead guitar is in open G and plays first position G licks the first time around. The next 8 bars are played at the 12th fret; the last time around, the solo is chord-based.

TRACK #2: SLOW 8-bar BLUES IN D

play 3 times

1	2	3	4	5	6	7	8
𝄆 D9	𝄎	G9	𝄎	D9	A7	D9	A7 𝄇

Again, there are three passes at this standard progression. The D-tuned lead guitar plays first position licks the first time, 12th fret licks the second time, and chord-based licks the third time.

TRACK #3: 12-bar BLUES SHUFFLE IN E
Three times around, the lead guitar plays Muddy Waters-style licks in standard tuning, as in **ROADMAP #9**.

TRACK#4: COUNTRY/ROCK TUNE IN C

This 8-bar progression repeats three times:

play 3 times

1	2	3	4	5	6	7	8
𝄆 C	𝄎	D	𝄎	F	𝄎	C	G 𝄇

The lead guitar is in standard tuning, using the concepts in Roadmap #10. The first time around consists mostly of C position playing; the second and third times the guitar changes positions with the tune's chord changes.

TRACK#5: ROCK TUNE IN G

The lead guitar, in standard tuning, plays G blues box slide licks, as in **ROADMAP #11**.

1	2	3	4	5	6	7	8
𝄆 G	𝄎	F	𝄎	C/E	𝄎	E♭	D 𝄇

During the bridge, the guitar switches to the positions outlined in **ROADMAP #10**, following the song's chord changes. Here's the progression:

Bridge

1	2	3	4	5	6	7	8
𝄆 C	𝄎	𝄎	𝄎	E♭	𝄎	F	𝄎 𝄇